Contents

Introduction

Reading the text of *Environment Today*, you become aware just how many academic disciplines are concerned with environmental issues, from biology, chemistry, physics and agriculture to economics, international relations and politics. For this reason the book is not just appropriate for a specific group of students and is truly interdisciplinary. As the author, Dr. Greenhalgh, stresses in her text, current environmental issues impinge crucially on everybody's life and therefore this book is bound to be of great interest, relevance and value to the general student of English as well as to those studying specific academic fields in the sciences and social sciences.

The text comprises 20 chapters with accompanying exercises. Before reading the chapter there is always a pre-reading activity for students to do. This is to prepare them for the content they are about to tackle by exploiting their knowledge, background and imagination in relation to it. For any classroom teacher of English, it is clearly necessary to have a warm-up and focus activity prior to dealing with a reading text. If, therefore the pre-reading section is omitted, it is methodologically sensible for teachers to introduce a pre-reading activity of their own so that the students do not handle the text cold in class without any focus for their reading.

The other common element in the exercises of each chapter is summary work. Reading efficiently to get the gist is a vital skill for any student of English. Similarly, many students will also be involved in writing a paper in English in their particular field and preparing a synopsis of the content. Each chapter contains written summary practice to provide training in this essential skill. The summary work takes a variety of forms, but is always structured so as to enable students to produce a competent, accurate paragraph of English. In this way they become familiar with how sentences are connected with each other and are developed logically into the sequence of a paragraph on a particular theme. A model summary is also provided with which students can compare their version.

1 Environmental damage through history

Pre-reading
Working in pairs or a small group, discuss the main factors which have had a negative effect on the environment during the last two hundred years. Then scan the text to find the main factors given by the author and compare them with your discussion.

The world has reached a crisis point. Our modern lifestyle is destroying the fragile environment. Most of this book is about what is happening to the environment today. This chapter is about our ancestors in past civilizations. We tend to imagine that ancient people were "environmentally friendly" and lived in harmony with nature. Some people (such as the American Indians) did indeed respect and protect their environment. But there are many historical examples of ancient people who destroyed the land they inhabited. In doing this, some of them destroyed their own livelihood.

Chapter 3 describes the **destruction of the rainforests**. Many communities today burn down trees to clear land for growing crops. Some of the earliest human communities also burned large areas of woodland for this purpose. Human societies evolved from small groups of hunter-gatherers to larger societies based around agriculture and domestic animals. According to many anthropologists, this was the beginning of "civilization." But it was also the beginning of mankind's destructive influence on the environment. We probably discovered how to manipulate fire about a million years ago. Until that time, most of the earth's land surface was covered in thick forests. Large forest fires, probably started deliberately by humans, created a new type of landscape in many parts of the world — the **savannah** or scrubland. The world's population then was only five or ten million. But these people literally changed the face of the earth. Several centuries later, the inhabitants of Easter Island in the Pacific Ocean cut down all their trees in order to erect huge religious statues. The islanders apparently forgot that the trees were their major source of food, fuel and shelter. Within a few years, the rich and sophisticated society on Easter Island was reduced to destitution and starvation.

Chapter 5 describes the threat of **extinction**, which affects many animal and plant species in the world today, and Chapter 19 gives examples of unnecessary cruelty to animals. We first demonstrated our ability to eradicate other species several centuries ago. The dodo (Fig. 1) was a large bird, rather like a turkey, that lived on the island of Mauritius in the Indian Ocean. The bird had no natural predators and never developed the ability to fly. Despite this, the dodo population thrived on the island for thousands of years. When the first humans arrived in Mauritius in the early 16th century, they found that the dodos were very tame. The birds walked right up to the human settlers and did not try to run away. The settlers killed the dodos, partly for food and partly for sport. By 1680, less than 200 years after the first human settlement on Mauritius, the last dodo was dead. Only the expression "as dead as a dodo" lives on in the English language.

Figure 1.1 *The dodo.*

Other animals who suffered at the hands of our ancestors include the **elephant** and the **buffalo**. Thousands of years ago, elephants walked freely over much of the earth. Elephant hunting by humans, mainly for the ivory trade, eliminated the elephant population from the Middle East and North Africa several centuries ago. The great explorer Marco Polo discovered a lucrative market for ivory in China because the Chinese had already killed all their own elephants. The European explorers who settled in the Americas spent several centuries trying to eradicate the native American Indian population. In the 19th century, they deliberately set out to kill all the buffalo in North America, because the Indians ate buffalo meat and used the hide of the buffalo for making clothes and shelters. In 1800, there were more than 60 million buffalo in the United States; by 1890 there were just 1,000 animals left. Today, the buffalo remains an endangered species (Fig. 2).

Figure 1.2 *North American buffalo.*

Chapter 9 describes the damage that modern man has done to the soil by intensive farming methods. One problem is **salinization** from excessive irrigation. But salinization is not entirely a problem of modern, high-technology agriculture. Our ancestors probably discovered irrigation about 5,500 years ago. The ancient Mesopotamians, who lived about 4,500 years ago, were enthusiastic farmers. They built extensive irrigation channels in river valleys to try to increase their crop yields. Unfortunately, this led to waterlogging and salinization of the soil. The yield of the staple crop, barley, fell dramatically and a prolonged famine occurred. The people who survived the famine had to change their staple crop from barley to wheat, which tolerated the salty soil better. The problem of **soil erosion**, which is also discussed in Chapter 9, has occurred ever since man began to destroy forests. There is geological evidence that a rapid increase in the rate of soil erosion occurred about 4,000 years ago in the northern European countries, particularly Britain, France and Germany. There was also an increase in silt deposits in rivers. The

time of this change corresponds to the introduction of agriculture to Europe. The destruction of forests, together with ancient man's agricultural methods, almost certainly caused this environmental damage.
Chapters 15 and 16 describe the problems of urban expansion, industrial pollution and waste disposal. Of course, these are largely the problems of an overpopulated world in the 20th century. But ever since humans first tried to live together in towns, there have been problems providing food, fuel, water and sanitation for urban communities. The great city of Ur (the biblical home of Abraham) was partially destroyed by floods after the inhabitants removed the trees around the headwaters of the river Euphrates to use as fuel for their fires. Although the Bible says that the cause of the flood was the anger of God, the real cause was probably environmental damage by man. Until less than a century ago, disposal of sewage was so inefficient that diseases such as cholera were endemic in many towns. With very few exceptions, urban communities used rivers and lakes as lavatories and garbage dumps. The ancient Romans, who understood the connection between sewage and disease, built their famous aqueducts to take the waste out of the city center (Fig. 3). But the aqueducts simply transported raw sewage to the countryside and dumped it there! The ancient Romans were pioneers of public health but they were very short-sighted about the health of the environment.

Figure 1.3 *Roman aqueducts.*

Environmentalists often claim that modern people are selfish, but modern people are probably no more selfish than most of their predecessors. However, there are two important differences between ancient civilizations and the world today. First, there are so many more people in the world today. We no longer live in isolated communities many hundreds of miles from our neighbors. The world is now a **global village**. As Chapter 2 explains, world population is reaching critical levels. Second, during the past 200 years, humankind has invented powerful technology that multiplies each individual's destructive impact on the environment. One man with an ax can cut down one or two large trees in a day; with modern machinery the same man can cut down a whole forest. Population growth and modern technology mean that we cannot afford to repeat the mistakes of our ancestors. The environmental crisis we are facing today will not just destroy a tiny corner of the earth. If we do not take action soon, it may cause irreversible damage to the entire planet.

Exercises

Section A

Read through the chapter carefully. Then complete the following to make suitable sentences according to the meaning of the chapter.

1 Man first began to destroy the environment when ....
....

2 A million years ago the size of the world's population was ....
....

3 The reason why the inhabitants of Easter Island cut down their trees was ....

4 The dodo became extinct because settlers on Mauritius
....

5 Elephants were common in most parts of the world ....
....

6 In the space of ninety years the number of buffalo in the U.S.A. decreased from ....
....

7 Salinization means that the soil ....
....

8 When man started to destroy forests, soil erosion ....
....

9 Poor sewage disposal has always caused ....
....

10 The surprising thing about Roman aqueducts was that ....
....

11 If nothing is done about the environmental crisis today, ...
....

12 During the last two hundred years the two main factors which have destroyed the environment are ....
....

Section B Summary Writing

Working with your partner, rearrange and write the following sentences in a paragraph that summarizes Chapter 1. Begin your paragraph with sentence 7. When you have finished, compare your own version with the final paragraph of the chapter.

1 There are, however, two important differences between ancient civilizations and the world today.
2 Second, during the past two hundred years, humankind has invented powerful technology which multiplies each individual's destructive impact on the environment.
3 If we do not take action soon, it may cause irreversible damage to the entire planet.
4 One man with an ax can cut down one or two large trees in a day; with modern machinery, the same man can cut down a whole forest.
5 The environmental crisis we are facing today will not just destroy a tiny corner of the earth.
6 We no longer live in isolated communities many hundreds of miles from our neighbors.
7 Modern people are selfish, but probably no more selfish than most of their predecessors.
8 First, there are so many more people in the world today.
9 Population growth and modern technology mean that we cannot afford to repeat the mistakes of our ancestors.

2 Population

Pre-reading

Working in pairs or a small group, try and answer the following questions before you read the chapter. Don't be afraid of guessing the answers! When you have finished, check your answers by reading the text.

1 The population of the world doubles
   a every 19 years.
   b every 39 years.
   c every 59 years.
   d every 99 years.
2 In 1987 the world population was
   a 5 billion people.
   b 15 billion people.
   c 25 billion people.
   d 30 billion people.
3 Nowadays the number of undernourished people in the world is
   a a quarter of the population.
   b a third of the population.
   c half of the population.
   d three quarters of the population.
4 In the United States the birth rate is about
   a 1.5.
   b 2.1.
   c 3.1.
   d 4.1.
5 The birth rate in Europe
   a is the same as in the United States.
   b is higher than in the United States.
   c is lower than in the United States.

6 By the year 2000 it is expected that most of the world's population will be in
a Africa.
b Europe.
c Asia.
d China.

7 In 1979 the Chinese government said that there should be
a no more children if possible.
b one-child families.
c a maximum of two children per family.
d the same number of children as before.

8 The population of China is
a 500 million.
b just less than a billion.
c more than a billion.
d two billion.

9 Nowadays Europe's population is falling.
True/False

10 Poor people in the world use more resources than rich people.
True/False

11 Educating women means reducing the growth of population.
True/False

12 Half of all abortions in the world are illegal.
True/False

13 Most Chinese families prefer to have a female child.
True/False

14 Poor people normally have more children than rich people.
True/False

15 A birth rate of 2.1 per woman means that the population does not change.
True/False

The world's population grows **exponentially**, and not arithmetically. It is important to understand what this means. Imagine that you have a very large box, and you put one grain of sand in the box every second. After five hundred years, the box is half full. It will take another five hundred years to fill the box completely. That is arithmetic growth. Now imagine that you are filling another large box with sand. This time you begin slowly. In the first year, you put in one grain; in the next year, two grains; in the next year, four grains; and so on. Each year, you double the amount of sand you put into the box. If it takes five hundred years to half fill *this* box, how long will it take to fill the box completely? The answer is one more year. That is exponential growth. These two types of growth are illustrated in Fig. 1.

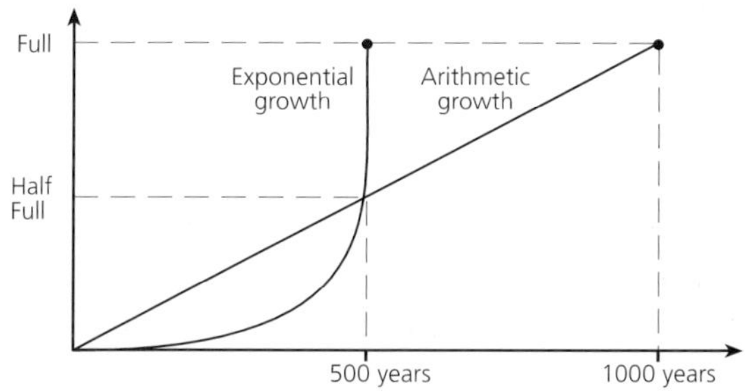

Figure 2.1 *Arithmetic and exponential growth.*

The population of the world doubles every 39 years. On July 11, 1987, it officially reached five billion people. Humans have been on Earth for about 35,000 years. But it will only take 39 years to add another five billion people. To accommodate all the extra people, everything in the world must double. For every house in the world today, we must build another house. For every field that we now use to grow crops, we will need another field, and for every reservoir of water, another reservoir. But the world is already critically short of food and water, and half the people in the world are already undernourished. If you take a few bacteria and put them on a plate of agar (which is their food supply), the number of bacteria will increase exponentially. Eventually the whole plate will be covered with bacteria.

But the number of bacteria does not level off when the food supply becomes limited. It falls dramatically because almost all the organisms suddenly die (Fig. 2). The same thing happens when populations of animals or plants outgrow their food supply. If we do not control human population growth, we risk a sudden catastrophic fall in the population as millions of people die.

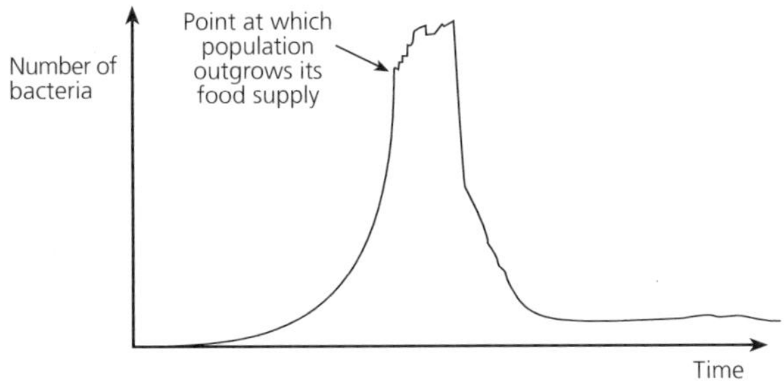

Figure 2.2 *Growth of bacteria on a limited food supply, showing catastrophic fall in population numbers when food supply becomes critical.*

Other resources as well as food are limited. Chapter 12 describes how our main energy source, fossil fuels, will run out within the next few decades. All the environmental problems discussed in this book (such as destruction of the rainforests, land degradation, pollution of air and water, urban expansion, and traffic congestion) have reached crisis point because the human population has reached crisis point. Every minute, 274 more people are born, but only 97 people die. Every minute the world gains 177 more consumers of energy, producers of sewage and, perhaps, future drivers of cars. And the population increase is occurring almost exclusively in the developing countries. If the birth rate (that is, the average number of children born to each woman) is 2.1, the total number of people will stay the same. The birth rate in the United States is now close to 2.1, and in Europe it is only 1.7. But Europe's population is not falling, because of immigration from the developing countries. The birth rate in Asia and Africa is between 3.5 and 4.2. Table 1 shows that Africans will increase from 8.9 percent of the world's population in 1950 to nearly 20 percent in 2025 if today's trends continue. Europeans will fall from 15.6 percent to 6.4 percent.

Today's trends may not continue, however. Several developing countries have already reduced their birth rates to much lower levels.

The most famous example is China. China already contains more than a billion people. The Chinese government reduced the birth rate from 4.74 to 2.36 in just 10 years between 1973 and 1983 by making **family planning** a "civic duty." The government rewarded families who had fewer children. They provided better quality housing, free child care and better schools for the children of small families. They gave people free time off work for abortion and sterilization. In 1979, the Chinese government declared that everyone should aim for a one-child family. Some people say that these policies are an infringement of human rights. Sometimes, the children suffer. Most Chinese families prefer to have a male child. Since the one-child family policy began, there have undoubtedly been many cases of female infanticide (that is, secretly murdering girl babies at birth) so that the mother can try again for a boy.

	1950	1985	2000	2025
Africa	8.9%	11.5%	14.2%	19.7%
Asia	54.7%	58.3%	58.0%	55.3%
China	22.1%	21.9%	20.5%	18.0%
Europe	15.6%	10.2%	8.4%	6.4%
USA	6.0%	4.9%	4.4%	3.8%

Table 1: Proportion of world population in different regions 1950 2025 (projected)

(source: United Nations Department of International Economic and Social Affairs: World Population at the Turn of the Century. New York, United Nations, 1989.)

Rich people use many times more resources than poor people. One American baby born today will probably consume as much energy as 50 to 100 Indian babies in his or her lifetime. Perhaps this is why the Third World poor have so bitterly resented the "population control programs" introduced by agencies from the richer nations. According to one rumor, American doctors injected thousands of Indian women with a contraceptive and told them that it was an anti-tetanus immunization. Another rumor says that the doctors gave away a radio to every man who was sterilized. Even if these rumors are untrue, they reflect the widespread public suspicion of family planning campaigns organized by foreign agencies. Despite this, many people in the Third World want contraception. Fifty percent of married women in developing countries do not want any more children. One child in three born in the developing world was an unwanted pregnancy. Worldwide, 40 million abortions take place every year, and half of these are done illegally. Illegal abortions are often painful and unsafe. Between 20,000 and 200,000 women in the world die every year as a result of having an abortion. In addition, one African woman in 14 dies in childbirth. Preventing unwanted pregnancies will also reduce the tragic deaths of many young mothers in the developing world.

Contraception is occasionally unacceptable for religious or cultural reasons. The Catholic church, which has an important influence in many developing countries (particularly South America), teaches that contraception is against God's will. In some male-dominated societies, women have few rights. Even if the woman wants to use contraception, her husband can overrule her wishes. The woman's status in society may depend on how many sons she has. In certain cultures, people think that children are a gift from God and that infertility is a punishment from the devil. Even well-educated people occasionally believe that using contraceptives will cause cancer, mental illness or loss of virility. Such prejudices will not change overnight.

As well as the availability of contraception, two other factors influence the number of children in a family: poverty and ignorance. Poor people usually have more children than rich people, for three reasons. First, poor parents know that their children are more likely to die. Every year, 15 million children in the world die before they reach the age of five. Most of these deaths are from preventable diseases, caused by overcrowding and malnutrition, such as diarrhea, tuberculosis and measles. Second, the children's labor can improve the family's income. An ancient proverb says, "a child has one mouth, but two hands." Children who are only four or five years old often work all day in the fields. Third, children are an "insurance policy" for old age. Most poor countries have no social security system. Old people depend on their children to keep them from destitution.

The education of women is another important influence on family size. Many infant deaths can be prevented by teaching nutrition and hygiene to the mothers. People cannot use effective contraceptives if they do not know that contraceptives exist. In the south Indian state of Kerala, the quality of basic health care and education has greatly improved over the past 30 years. Infant mortality is much lower than the national average, and female literacy is very high. People in Kerala usually respond positively to health education and family planning campaigns. Kerala's population is now almost stable, even though it is one of the poorest states in India and all family planning has been entirely voluntary.

The United Nations organization UNICEF has identified four essential measures for controlling population growth: providing contraceptives, reducing poverty, improving the health and education of women, and decreasing child mortality. As Chapter 18 argues, many of the world's environmental problems are rooted in poverty. The population explosion is no exception. One way or another, the exponential growth of the world's population will soon end. Hopefully, the cause will be a planned and voluntary reduction in the birth rate rather than a catastrophic increase in deaths from overcrowding and starvation.

Exercises

Section A Summary Writing

Read the following paragraph, which is a summary of the essential points of the chapter. Complete it by putting one word in each of the blank spaces.

Because the world's population grows exponentially, this .... that at the present rate it .... every thirty-nine years. However, the .... of the world are limited, so .... is a serious risk of .... of people dying, especially in developing .... Possibly these trends may not continue .... the future because some countries, for .... China, have already reduced their birth rates. Yet .... the need for contraception, population control programs .... often rejected by poor developing countries .... a variety of reasons. According to UNICEF .... four main ways of controlling the .... of population are: providing contraceptives, reducing .... , improving the health and education of .... and decreasing child mortality.

Section B Discussion Work

i) Discuss the population trends in your own country, the reasons for those trends and the effects on people's lives.

ii) "The policy of the Chinese government regarding family planning cannot be accepted in any way." Discuss this question in a small group and report your opinions to the rest of the class.

3 The destruction of the rainforests

Pre-reading

With a partner, consider the following questions and try to answer them. Then quickly scan the opening paragraph of the chapter to check your answers.

1 Where are the rainforests in the world?
2 Where are the largest rainforests found?
3 If the present trend of destroying the rainforests continues, how long do you think it will take to destroy them all?

The tropical rainforests surround the equator of the earth like a belt. They occupy a total area of about nine million square kilometers. The largest rainforests are in South America, particularly the Amazon forest in Brazil which stretches to Peru, Ecuador, Colombia, Venezuela and French Guyana (Fig. 1). Smaller forests are found in tropical Asia and central Africa. The rainforests are rapidly being cut down. Nobody knows exactly how much is cut down every year. Estimates vary between 100,000 and 400,000 square kilometers. Brazil alone lost about 48,000 square kilometers of rainforest in 1990. The tropical forests of west Africa (Nigeria and the Ivory Coast) have almost disappeared over the past 40 years. According to the most conservative estimate, all the rainforests in the world will be gone in less than a century unless the rate of felling slows down. A more realistic estimate is 30 years.

Figure 3.1 *Tropical rainforest in Venezuela.*

Why are people cutting down the rainforests? Between 10 and 30 percent of the trees are sold as logs to the timber trade. Most of the trees from the Nigerian rainforests were sold to the timber industry in Japan, the United States and other industrialized countries. Tropical hardwoods such as mahogany are strong, attractive and hardwearing. They are used in rich countries to make luxury furniture, doors and window frames. But much of the wood is not made into durable products. It is made into cheap, throwaway goods. A large proportion of the hardwood imported into Japan in recent years has been made into plywood, paper or chopsticks. The destruction of rainforests for the timber trade sometimes involves political corruption. In many developing countries, a person must get a license from the government before he can cut down trees. A license to cut down trees is almost a license to print money. Government officials sometimes give out these licenses to members of their own families or in return for "favors" from business people. In the countries where this kind of corruption occurs, politicians will be reluctant to restrict the activity of timber traders.

The multinational timber companies often make roads deep into the forests so that they can drag the logs away. They may only cut down a few trees themselves, but their roads make the forests accessible to local peasant farmers. These farmers cut down trees to create new cropland, or even simply for fuel. It is a great tragedy that large areas of the Amazon rainforests have been wasted as firewood! Tree felling for firewood is also a problem in the temperate forests. Over 85 percent of all the wood cut in the Third World (hardwood and softwood) is used for fuel. Wood provides more energy in the developing world today than the total energy from fossil fuels, nuclear fuels and alternative energy sources.

The largest cause of the destruction of rainforests is probably the creation of grazing land to feed cattle. The growth of the fast food industry in the 1970s created a demand for cheap beef for making hamburgers (see Chapter 10). In the late 1970s, in return for a large loan from the international banks (see Chapter 18), the Costa Rican government removed thousands of hectares of rainforest by the infamous **slash-and-burn** technique to provide grazing land for export cattle. Other countries soon saw the profit they could make from cattle farming and began to cut down their own rainforests. According to one estimate, half of the world's rainforests have already been cut down to make space for the meat industry, and approximately half a metric ton of vegetation is destroyed for every hamburger eaten.

Why do we need to conserve the rainforests? First, because the rainforests are the lungs of the world. They take in carbon dioxide and give out oxygen by photosynthesis:

CO_2 + H_2O + light energy ————> CHO + O_2
carbon dioxide + water + sunlight ————> carbohydrate + oxygen

The loss of vegetation in the rainforests magnifies the greenhouse effect. As Chapter 6 describes, we are producing more and more carbon dioxide from burning fossil fuels. The capacity of the rainforests to absorb this environmentally toxic gas is becoming ever more crucial. Second, the rainforests are the world's most important means of storing water. The trees soak up water in the rainy season and slowly release it into the ground and rivers. This protects the fragile soils from the potentially devastating effects of tropical storms. The rainforests supply water to the rivers during the dry season. If they did not do this, many rivers would disappear in the dry season and become raging torrents in the rainy season, flooding the nearby fields and washing away the soil.

Third, the rainforests control the **climate**. Seventy-five percent of the rain that falls on the tropical rainforests enters the trees from the soil by transpiration and then evaporates from the surface of the leaves. (The other 25 percent of the rainwater stays in the soil and enters the rivers as run-off). These two processes are known together as "evapotranspiration." The heat energy required to evaporate the water from the forests cools the equatorial regions. The clouds formed by the water vapor also cool the land by reflecting solar radiation back into space. These clouds are carried to cooler parts of the earth by natural convection, where they release warm rain which raises the temperature in these areas. If the rainforests disappear, so will the rain. Without the rainforests, the temperature difference between the tropics and the temperate zones would be far greater.

Fourth, the rainforests are a reservoir of **micronutrients**. Tropical rainforests usually grow on poor soil. Most of the essential nutrients are stored not in the soil but within the trees themselves. The roots of the trees, which make up about 60 percent of their mass, do not grow deep into the soil. They spread out and form a thick network a few meters beneath the surface. These shallow roots absorb free nutrients released from the thick layer of decaying vegetation on the forest floor. Recycling of these nutrients is crucial to the survival of the ecosystem that the rainforests support. When the trees are cut down, vital nutrients are washed away with the run-off and a whole ecosystem quickly dies.

Fifth, the rainforests, and the ecosystems that they support, are an important source of **raw materials** for many different industries. They supply us with hundreds of useful products — from rubber to peanuts. One very important benefit is the supply of **medicinal plants**. About 80 percent of all traditional herbal medicines and 25 percent of modern Western medicines are extracted from plants that grow in the rainforests. We do not know how many more important medicines are lying undiscovered within the rainforests. Scientists and ecologists are working together in this important branch of medical research. Loss of plant species within the rainforests (see Chapter 5) will mean that many lifesaving drugs will never be discovered. One last — and very important — reason for conserving the rainforests is that they are the home of several million people, who still live in primitive tribal societies within the forests (Fig. 2). We have both a moral and a scientific duty to protect the homelands of these unique and fascinating societies. The rainforest tribes have an intimate knowledge of the many thousands of plants and animals that live there. They can show us how to use these plants and animals for new sources of food, medicines and building materials. The tribal people are more than an anthropological curiosity. They are the key to the living resources of the rainforests.

Figure 3.2 *Indigenous people of the tropical rainforests.*

Exercises

Summary Writing

How many reasons does the author give for conserving the rainforests? What are they? Check the answers you noted with the ones in the following four sentences. Finally, rearrange and write out the four sentences so that they form a summary of the points given in the chapter.

1 Moreover, one other benefit relates to the supply of many raw materials, products and medicinal plants.
2 Finally, the homes of millions of people are to be found in the rainforests and this homeland should be protected for moral and scientific reasons.
3 They act as the lungs and watersheds of the world, they control the climate and are a reservoir of micronutrients.
4 There are a number of reasons why the rainforests should be conserved.

4 Saving the rainforests

> *Pre-reading*
> In a small group try to think of ways of saving the rainforests. What can be done in rich, developed countries and what can the developing countries do? Report your views to the rest of the class and when all your ideas have been collected, compare your views with those of the author.

The previous chapter described how we are rapidly destroying the tropical rainforests. What can we do to conserve what is left of them? One important step is to reduce the demand for new hardwood products. Governments could do this by putting a high tax on these products. The revenue from a **tropical hardwood** tax could fund conservation projects. So far, governments have been reluctant to introduce a tax on hardwood. Like all new taxes, it would make the government unpopular! In fact, until recently, certain Third World countries (notably Brazil) had a tax system that encouraged the destruction of the rainforests. They were so keen to promote the export of cattle that they offered tax *concessions* to the farmers who burned the forests! Most of these schemes have now been abolished. The demand for hardwood in the West is falling even without a tropical hardwood tax. The international timber trade has received a lot of bad publicity because of its role in the destruction of the rainforests. Many environmentally-conscious people today refuse to buy goods that are made from tropical hardwoods. Some timber companies now concentrate on selling softwoods such as pine and beech instead. Other companies recycle hardwood by taking apart old furniture. A few companies still cut down hardwood trees but they are also planting new trees to try to rebuild the forests. However, no timber company has yet achieved the goal of **sustainable timber extraction** (that is, replacing as many trees as it cuts down) in the tropical rainforests.

Restricting the activities of the timber trade will not, on its own, save the rainforests. We must also address the other causes of deforestation — lack of alternative fuel, the need to create grazing land for cattle and the widespread public ignorance about the ecological importance of the rainforests. In 1987, several international organizations (including the World Bank, the United Nations Food and Agriculture Organization, and the United Nations Development Program) launched the Tropical Forest Action Plan, a five-year plan to invest money in forestry, conservation and agricultural projects. Their aims were: to plant new hardwood forests, particularly in vital watershed zones; to provide alternative firewood supplies from fast-growing softwood trees (such as eucalyptus), to promote the practice of **agroforestry** (in which cattle graze within the forests so that farmers do not need to cut down trees); and to encourage research into conservation and forestry in the developing countries. The Tropical Forest Action Plan, and other similar projects, have made some progress toward reforestation. But environmentalists have criticized such projects for spending most of their money on building ugly plantations of fast-growing trees all of the same species. They spend only a small fraction of their funds on conserving the existing forests or on research. Their ultimate aim (according to critics) is to grow hardwood trees as a renewable cash crop, rather than to conserve the rainforests and the great diversity of plant and animal life within them. It takes about 150 years for a hardwood tree to reach maturity, but it takes many centuries for the full rainforest ecosystem to become established.

Figure 4.1 *Madagascar periwinkle.*

As Chapter 18 explains, conservation costs money. The developing countries cannot afford to forgo the immediate revenue that they can earn by selling timber or raising cattle. But they could, and should, try to develop the economic potential of the rich resources that grow beneath the trees—the **non-timber forest products**. The medicinal plants in the rainforests have great scientific potential, but they also have enormous economic value. Harvesting medicinal herbs for the pharmaceutical industry is potentially more profitable for the developing countries than selling timber or raising cattle on the deforested land. Fig. 1 shows the Madagascar periwinkle, a rainforest plant from which an important anti-cancer drug is extracted. The income from the sale of this drug in 1990 was about $50 million, but unfortunately most of the profits went to the pharmaceutical industry in the West rather than to the people of Madagascar. If the poor countries are to benefit from non-timber forest products, the distribution of profits must change radically. Everyone agrees, in theory, that the poor nations need financial incentives to conserve what is left of the rainforests, and that these incentives must come from the rich countries. But at the United Nations Conference on Environment and Development (UNCED) in Rio de Janeiro, 1992, delegates from rich and poor countries argued angrily with one another. The delegates from the rich countries agreed in principle with an action plan to save the rainforests, but in the end they were too greedy to sacrifice their own comfortable lifestyles. In addition, they did not trust the poor countries; they believed that money given for conservation projects would be wasted or stolen by incompetent and corrupt officials. Instead of an international treaty signed by all or most countries, UNCED only produced only a "statement of principles." The next few years will probably demonstrate that this statement is not worth the recycled paper it is printed on.

The plight of the disappearing tropical rainforests is one of the most urgent environmental crises in the world today. The "lungs of the world" are being sacrificed for the rich man's love of hardwood furniture and hamburgers, and the poor man's need for fuel and a basic income. Conserving the rainforests is an ecological imperative that demands personal sacrifices from rich and poor alike. The rich must change their consumption habits. The poor must find alternative sources of fuel and income so that they no longer need to plunder the precious rainforests to ensure their own survival. The destruction of the rainforests is an example of how poverty and environmental destruction are interdependent problems. Both require international dialogue and political action. The Tropical Forest Action Plan and the UNCED statement of principles have been relatively ineffective. In reality, the fight to save the rainforests has hardly begun.

Exercises

Summary Writing

i) When you have read through the chapter, decide with your partner which paragraph summarizes the whole content best.
ii) Complete the paragraph below by putting one word in each of the blank spaces and then check your version with the final paragraph in the chapter.

The plight of the disappearing tropical .... is one of the most urgent environmental crises .... the world today. The lungs of the world are .... sacrificed for the rich man's love .... hardwood furniture and hamburgers and the poor man's .... for fuel and a basic income. .... the rainforests is an ecological imperative .... demands personal sacrifices from rich and poor alike. The rich must .... their consumption habits. The poor must find alternative sources of fuel .... income so that they no longer need to plunder the precious rainforests to .... their own survival. The destruction of the rainforests is an example of .... poverty and environmental destruction are interdependent .... Both require international dialogue and political .... The Tropical Forest Action Plan and the UNCED statement of principles .... been relatively ineffective. In reality the fight to save the rainforests has .... begun.

5 Biodiversity and genetic resources

Pre-reading

With your partner try to match the definition with the correct word or phrase. Guess if you're not sure! Then scan the text quickly to see if you were right.

1 Biodiversity	a A plant that only lasts a year
2 A species	b An end to birth
3 Genetic resources	c Many different forms of life
4 A perennial	d A legal agreement between countries
5 An annual	e A plant that grows every year
6 Extinction	f A group of animals, plants or microorganisms sharing a common genetic structure
7 A treaty	g The great variety of different species of animals, plants and microorganisms
8 A predator	h Somebody or something that hunts

When we think of wildlife facing extinction, we are usually thinking of large majestic animals such as whales, elephants and rhinos (see Chapter 19) or of the "cuddly" black-and-white panda (Fig. 1). These creatures are indeed at risk of extinction because of irresponsible and cruel hunting by human predators. It is easy to become angry at the plight of these endearing mammals. But the threat of extinction is not limited to the few species that we can recognize in pictures or visit in zoos. The threat of extinction affects almost every species on earth, down to the tiniest microbe.

A **species** is a group of animals, plants or microorganisms that share a common genetic structure. Members of a species can mate with one another but not with members of another species. The earth probably contains between 10 and 100 million different species, although scientists have so far only identified 1.4 million of them. Each species is genetically unique. This means that we cannot

Figure 5.1 *The "cuddly" black and white panda.*

produce new members of a species by breeding other species. The great variety of different species of animals, plants and micro organisms are the world's genetic resources. There is a new word in the English language that underlines the importance of conserving these resources: biodiversity, which means biological diversity or, literally, "many different forms of life." Fifty to seventy percent of all the earth's animal, plant and bacteria species live in the tropical rainforests. The floor of the forest is a warm, moist, sheltered environment that encourages a great variety of living things to grow. Wild plants and animals in the rainforests already supply us with hundreds of useful materials, foods and medicines. The genetic resources within the rainforests provide a huge potential for new developments. We do not know very much about the balance of nature inside the rainforests. We cannot say that any single species is unimportant to the rest of the ecosystem. Maintaining biodiversity by conserving the rainforests is one of the greatest priorities for environmentalists today. Yet at the present rate of destruction, 7 percent of the earth's biodiversity is lost every 25 years.

The **balance of nature** within any ecosystem depends on the complex interaction between millions of species of animals, plants and micro-organisms. The death of one species could threaten the survival of hundreds of others. A second species might lose its food supply and it, too, might become extinct. Another species could lose its predators, so it might become more numerous. The populations of parasites and microorganisms that depend on these larger species will also change. This may lead to the spread of new, virulent diseases in the higher organisms. The balance of nature is often a very precarious one. There are many more species of small organisms than of large ones. Insects outnumber all other animal species combined, and bacteria outnumber all the animal and plant species together. These small organisms have a large influence on the microenvironment. Microorganisms influence important physical properties such as the acidity and mineral content of the soil, the salinity of the sea, and the amount of oxygen and carbon dioxide in the air. Changes in the populations of microorganisms may, therefore, cause major changes in the composition of the earth and its atmosphere.

In general, organisms that live in the wild are stronger and more resistant to disease than domestic strains. They can replace domestic strains that develop disease. In the 1860s, the grape vines in Europe were infested with a deadly pest, phylloxera, which threatened to destroy the entire European grape harvest. The wild American vines were resistant to phylloxera, so farmers cross-bred the European vines with these wild strains and the grape harvest survived. A more recent example of the benefits of biodiversity is a species of wild corn discovered a few years ago growing in a Mexican forest. The wild corn was extremely hardy and was resistant to viruses that often attack cultivated corn. The wild strain was a perennial (that is, it grew again spontaneously every year), whereas other forms of corn are annuals (that is, the farmers must sow new seeds every year). Scientists successfully cross-bred the wild strain with domestic varieties and created a new, hardy, perennial strain of cultivated corn. The wild Mexican corn was only growing in a tiny area of forest — about four hectares in total. When the corn was discovered, this small area was threatened by timber traders who were about to cut down the trees.

Today, scientists are trying to store wild strains of all the staple food crops in case the domestic strains develop disease. They have occasionally been successful. A few years ago a deadly virus, Yellow Dwarf Virus, spread through the barley crops in the United States. Scientists at the Center for Plant Genetics in Addis Ababa, Ethiopia, had stored wild strains of barley that were resistant to Yellow Dwarf

Virus. They sent some seeds to farmers in the U.S. and thereby prevented a complete failure of the harvest. But we cannot always rely on scientists to restore the balance of nature when it goes wrong. We cannot maintain biodiversity in the plant and animal worlds by storing every single species in laboratories. The world's ecosystem is far too complicated. The best place to store our genetic resources is in their natural habitat. We must try to conserve what is left of these habitats before it is too late.

Conserving biodiversity was one of the most controversial subjects of the UNCED conference in Rio de Janeiro in 1992. The genetic resources in the rainforests, coastal waters, and agricultural landscapes promise financial profits in future years if we invest money in protecting biodiversity today. But the developing countries, which own the rainforests, argued that most research into genetic resources will occur in the industrialized countries, which will protect their discoveries by patent, and most commercial benefits from these discoveries will go to multinational companies in the West. This is already the case for certain medicinal plants (see Chapter 4). The poor countries therefore demanded that the rich countries pay the full cost of the planned conservation and research programs. The UNCED conference produced the **biodiversity treaty** (a legal agreement between countries to protect wildlife and conserve genetic resources), but the delegates from the richest country in the world, the United States, refused to sign it because they thought that the financial liability for their country would be excessive.

Extinction is final. It does not just mean death; it means an end to birth. Once the last member of a species has died, that species is lost to the planet forever. Man has the power to upset the balance of nature but he does not have the power to restore that balance. This is why we must try to protect every living species on the earth — even the ugliest insects and the tiny, invisible, unglamorous bacteria. Of all the world's resources, its genetic resources are the least renewable of all.

Exercises

Paragraph Writing

Below are eight simple sentences about biodiversity and the Rio conference:

1 Conserving biodiversity was one of the subjects at the Rio conference in 1992.
2 Investing in biodiversity means profits in the future from genetic resources.
3 Developing countries wanted industrialized countries to pay for conservation and research.
4 Most research will be done in the developed world.
5 Huge western multinational companies will obtain the profits.
6 Finally a biodiversity treaty was produced.
7 The United States refused to sign it.
8 The United States would have to pay too much for the conservation and research.

Combine the eight sentences to make three complex sentences, and write the three sentences as a paragraph. You can join the simple sentences in the following way:

1 Join sentences 1 and 2 with *and*.
2 Join sentences 3, 4 and 5 with *because* and *and*.
3 Join sentences 6, 7 and 8 with *which* and *as*.

Finally, compare your paragraph with the one given in the Key to the Exercises at the back of the book.

6 The atmosphere (1): The ozone layer and the greenhouse effect

Pre-reading

In a small group discuss the current problems associated with the ozone layer and the greenhouse effect and make notes of your main points. Then compare your notes with the points made by the author.

The atmosphere is the layer of gas that surrounds the earth. The composition of the atmosphere changes with the distance from the earth's surface (Fig. 1). The layer near the surface—the **troposphere** —contains the air we breathe, which is 78 percent nitrogen (N_2), 21 percent oxygen (O_2), 0.03 percent carbon dioxide (CO_2), and 1 percent inert gases such as argon. Water vapor, small particles of dust, and tiny quantities of other gases such as helium, ozone (O_3), nitrous oxide (N_2O), and methane (CH_4), are also present. The **stratosphere** (between 15 and 80 kilometers above sea level) contains thin, cold air with less oxygen and no dust or water vapor. The **ionosphere** contains very thin air and electrically charged particles which reflect electromagnetic waves. We use the ionosphere to send radio signals around the earth.

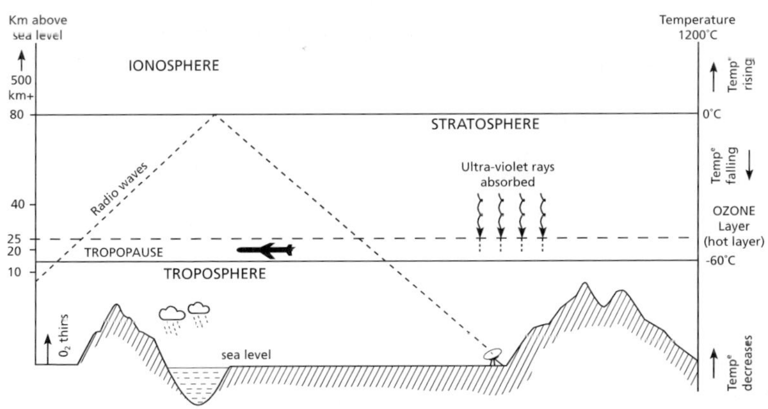

Figure 6.1 *The earth's atmosphere.*

The lower part of the stratosphere contains a band of warm gas called the **ozone layer** (between 15 and 40 kilometers above sea level). Ozone absorbs very shortwave ultraviolet radiation — that is, the harmful, burning rays from the sun. These rays kill plants and cause burns, skin cancer, and cataracts in animals and man. The ozone layer protects us from these damaging effects. The man-made chemicals **chlorofluorocarbons** (CFCs) break up ozone molecules. CFCs occur in some aerosols (such as deodorants, hair sprays and cleaning fluids), expanded polystyrene (such as fast-food packaging) and the cooling mechanism of refrigerators. Most scientists now accept that CFCs are very bad for the environment. They have already caused a large hole in the ozone layer (Fig. 2). CFCs also contribute to the greenhouse effect (see below). In 1987, 30 countries signed the Montreal Protocol, in which they agreed to cut production of CFCs by 50 percent before 1999. Several countries have since agreed to phase out CFCs completely. The manufacture of new products containing CFCs is slowly declining in most countries, but it is not happening quickly enough. Some environmentalists argue that governments should ban all production of CFCs immediately to prevent an irreversible environmental crisis.

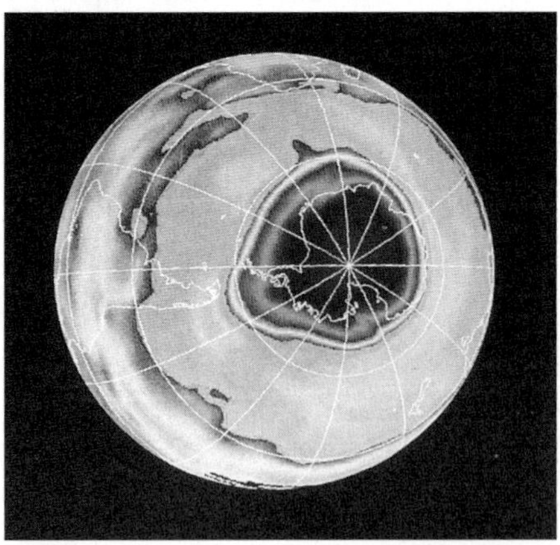

Figure 6.2 *Hole in the ozone layer caused by CFCs.*

Another environmental problem in the atmosphere is the **greenhouse effect**. Some gases transmit shortwave radiation but not longwave radiation. The sun's energy arrives as shortwave radiation; some of this is reflected away in the clouds and upper atmosphere and some is absorbed into the ground (Fig. 3). About 5 percent of the energy is reflected off the earth's surface as longwave radiation. Certain gases in the upper troposphere — especially carbon dioxide, methane and CFCs — reflect this longwave radiation back to earth. The glass in a greenhouse conserves heat by the same principle, so these gases are known as "greenhouse gases." The greenhouse effect is very important; if it did not occur at all, the temperature of the planet would be 40 degrees lower and the oceans would freeze. But an increase in the greenhouse effect (caused by an increase in the concentration of greenhouse gases in the atmosphere) may lead to **global warming**, with disastrous consequences.

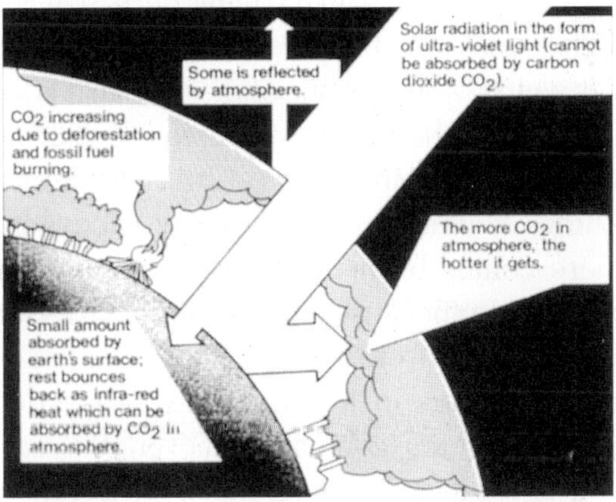

Figure 6.3 *The greenhouse effect.*

The higher average temperatures produced by global warming could cause dramatic changes in the weather. Less rain might fall over large land masses. Central Africa, south Asia and some parts of the United States could risk severe drought and famine. More rain might fall in coastal areas and over the oceans; there might be more storms and hurricanes in the Pacific. A rise in the earth's average temperature of only one or two degrees would probably melt large expanses of ice in the Arctic and the Antarctic (the polar ice caps) and raise sea levels. Sea levels throughout the world are already rising by about two millimeters a year. If the polar ice caps melt, sea levels could rise by more than a meter over a few decades. Many heavily populated regions, such as Bangladesh, the Nile delta, the Netherlands and Indonesia, would be permanently flooded. Cities are often found on the coast where a river meets the sea, so many of the world's major population centers could become uninhabitable. About one billion people would lose their homes and become **environmental refugees**. Some islands, such as the Maldives in the Pacific, might disappear completely.

Carbon dioxide accounts for 55 percent of the greenhouse effect; CFCs account for 17 percent; methane for 15 percent and nitrous oxide for 5 percent. Carbon dioxide occurs naturally in the atmosphere. It is produced when animals and plants respire (see Chapter 3). But "natural" carbon dioxide forms only 0.03 percent of the atmosphere. Higher concentrations of carbon dioxide are not natural at all. Carbon dioxide is also produced when living things burn, so it is a by-product of industrial processes which use fossil fuels (coal, gas or oil), and motor vehicles which burn gasoline or diesel fuel. It is also produced when volcanoes erupt and when tropical rainforests are cleared by burning (see Chapter 3). Methane is also a "natural" gas, produced when living things decompose in the absence of oxygen. Methane in the atmosphere comes from rotting vegetation, particularly rice fields, and from cattle (because bacteria in their intestines produce methane). It also comes from leaks in the extraction of natural gas (see Chapter 12). Methane in the atmosphere breaks down relatively quickly (in about 10 years, compared to over 100 years for carbon dioxide and CFCs), so it is a relatively minor environmental problem. However, some scientists believe that huge quantities of methane are trapped within the polar ice caps and will be released suddenly if the polar ice caps melt. This phenomenon would accelerate global warming. Nitrous oxide in the atmosphere comes from bacteria beneath the earth's surface, which convert nitrates in the soil to the gases nitrogen and nitrous oxide. The increased use of artificial fertilizers in recent years has increased the production of nitrous oxide. Levels of nitrous oxide in the air will continue to increase for many years, because there is already a large reservoir of artificial nitrates within the soil.

How can we stop the greenhouse effect from getting worse? The most important way is to reduce the emission of carbon dioxide by industry and motor vehicles. This is discussed in Chapters 12, 16 and 17. At the 1992 United Nations Conference on Environment and

Development in Rio de Janeiro, 150 countries signed the **climatic change treaty**, in which they agreed to work toward reducing global emissions of carbon dioxide by the turn of the century. However, delegates were worried that the changes would be expensive and inconvenient. Delegates from the United States refused to allow specific targets for reducing carbon dioxide emissions, so the treaty is little more than a general statement of principles.

We cannot see, hear, taste or smell the earth's atmosphere, but it provides vital oxygen, protects us from damaging solar radiation and stabilizes the earth's climate. Pollution has already caused a large hole in the ozone layer and increased global warming. Some people do not believe that CFCs are harmful. They are ignoring the scientific evidence. Some people argue that the phenomenon of global warming has not yet been proven beyond doubt. Temperatures vary between day and night (**diurnal variation**), between winter and summer (**seasonal variation**), and between different geographical regions (**regional variation**). It is difficult to prove that average temperatures throughout the world are half a degree higher than they were 50 years ago. But it is surely sensible to try to reduce emissions of greenhouse gases today, rather than wait for another 10 or 15 years until the phenomenon of global warming is absolutely certain. Reducing CFC production and greenhouse gas emission will cost money and compromise our comfortable lifestyle. But if we do not take action to protect the earth's atmosphere, it will soon become unable to protect us.

Exercises

Section A

After reading through the text carefully, say whether the following statements are true or false.

1 The air we breathe consists mainly of oxygen.
2 The air is thinner in the ionosphere than in the stratosphere.
3 Chlorofluorocarbons are the main factor in the greenhouse effect.

4 By breaking up ozone molecules, chlorofluorocarbons have caused a hole in the ozone layer.
5 Thirty countries have decided to phase out chlorofluorocarbons completely.
6 Nowadays there are fewer products containing chlorofluorocarbons.
7 Without the greenhouse effect the climate on the earth would be much colder.
8 The sun's energy reaches the earth as infra-red radiation.
9 Because of global warming there is now a risk of drought and famine in parts of Africa and Asia.
10 If there is a rise in temperature of one or two degrees, the sea level will rise by about 2 millimeters a year.

Section B Summary Writing

The following paragraph describes the greenhouse effect but the verbs have been omitted. Rewrite the paragraph, putting the verbs in the correct form. You may have to use a verb more than once. The verbs you can use are: *to know, to reflect, to absorb, to arrive, to conserve, to occur, to be, to freeze, to transmit*. Finally, check your version with the third paragraph in the chapter.

<u>The Greenhouse Effect</u>

Another environmental problem is the greenhouse effect. Some gases .... shortwave radiation but not longwave radiation. The sun's energy .... as shortwave radiation; some of this .... away in the clouds and upper atmosphere and some .... into the ground. About 5 percent of the energy .... off the earth's surface as longwave radiation. Certain gases in the upper troposphere—especially carbon dioxide, methane and CFCs— .... this longwave radiation back to the earth. The glass in a greenhouse .... heat by the same principle, so these gases .... as "greenhouse gases". The greenhouse effect .... very important; if it did not .... at all, the temperature of the planet .... 40 degrees lower and the oceans ....

7 The atmosphere (2): air pollution

> *Pre-reading*
> What causes air pollution? Discuss this question with your partner and make a list of the main things which you think cause air pollution. Then compare your list with the factors mentioned by the author.

In the past, air pollution in industrialized countries caused a visible haze called **smog** (Fig. 1). Smog is a mixture of different pollutants (mainly sulphur dioxide gas and particles of soot) and water vapor in still, cold air. It occurs in unusual weather conditions when there is **temperature inversion** — that is, a layer of cold air close to the ground with a layer of warmer air above it. In normal weather conditions, air near the ground is warmer than air higher up; warm air rises and the air circulates. With temperature inversion, the air does not circulate so pollutants become trapped close to the ground. When these pollutants combine with fog, they form a visible suspension in the air; this is known as smog. The main sources of sulphur dioxide and soot are **fossil fuels**, particularly coal. Oil, natural gas and hard, black coal produce much less sulphur dioxide than soft, brown coal (see Chapter 12). Brown coal is cheap and plentiful in Eastern Europe and in many developing countries. Sulphur-based smog rarely occurs in developed countries today, but it is a major source of pollution in newly-industrializing countries such as India and China (see Chapter 17). Sulphur dioxide is, incidentally, also emitted from volcanoes when they erupt; this "natural" sulphur dioxide can cause the same environmental problems as industrial emissions. Fortunately, volcanoes do not erupt very often!

Figure 7.1 *Smog in London.*

Smog is very bad for health. Water vapor combines with sulphur dioxide to form **sulphuric acid** and with nitrogen monoxide to form **nitric acid**. These acids irritate the lungs. In the famous London smog of 1952, about 4,000 people (mostly infants and the elderly) died in two weeks from chest diseases such as bronchitis and pneumonia. In 1956, the British government introduced legislation against air pollution—the Clean Air Act. It became illegal to burn coal or wood in residential areas. People had to use smokeless fuel such as gas or electricity. The Clean Air Act also said that industries must build tall chimneys to release their waste high into the atmosphere. This was a short-sighted policy, because the industries were not required to improve their production processes. Industrial pollution in Britain did not decrease after the Clean Air Act; it was simply released into the upper atmosphere. Air pollution in the upper atmosphere does not cause smog, but it has other harmful effects. Sulphuric and nitric acids are carried long distances with air currents and become **acid rain**. Acid rain damages crops and forests, destroys aquatic life in lakes and rivers, and ruins buildings. The timber and fishing industries in Sweden have suffered badly because of acid rain originating in British factories and power stations. Trees have died, and lakes that were once full of plants and fish are now devoid of all life. In sandstone or limestone regions, certain chemicals within the rock (such as calcium carbonate) will reduce the acidity of the water. This is called **natural buffering**. But if the lake lies on an insoluble or acidic rock such as granite, no natural buffering will occur and the acidity of the water will remain high. Scientists have tried to reduce the acidity of lakes artificially by adding chemicals to the water, but this intended remedy sometimes upsets the ecological balance even further. Acid rain destroys buildings by corroding metal and dissolving stone; some important historical monuments are being washed away by acid rain.

The ozone layer in the upper atmosphere protects us from solar radiation, but **ozone** at ground level is a major air pollutant. It causes chest disease, particularly asthma, and irritates the eyes and skin. Ozone at ground level comes from motor vehicles. Hydrocarbons and nitrogen oxides in vehicle exhausts combine with one another in sunlight to produce ozone. This **photochemical smog** is worst in traffic-congested cities on hot, dry summer days, whereas sulphur-based smog occurs on cold, damp winter days. Photochemical smog is especially common when the vehicle engines are old and poorly maintained, as often occurs in developing countries. Old-fashioned diesel engines are a particular problem. In some overpopulated cities such as Mexico City and São Paulo, almost all children suffer from coughs and wheezing; this is mainly due to the effects of ozone and other motor vehicle pollutants. In the summer of 1990, the air in Mexico City became so heavily polluted that birds dropped dead in the parks. The government declared a state of emergency and closed schools and public places for several days. The toxic emissions from car exhausts can be reduced considerably by installing **catalytic converters** on the engines. These devices are now compulsory in new cars in many developed countries, but they are rarely found in developing countries. Traffic pollution is discussed in Chapter 17.

Another toxic component of car exhaust fumes is **lead**. Until quite recently, all gasoline contained a lead-based compound (tetraethyl lead) which made the gasoline burn more smoothly. Lead is a very poisonous metal. Human beings cannot excrete lead, so it accumulates in the body. Even in tiny concentrations (25 milligrams per liter), it can cause headaches, abdominal pains, miscarriages and general tiredness. Lead is particularly toxic to growing brain cells. Lead pollution from car exhaust probably reduces the intelligence of children who live in crowded cities. Today, more and more cars are made to run on unleaded gasoline. All new cars produced in the United States, Britain and many other developed countries must now run on unleaded gasoline. Lead is also found in old water pipes and old paints. Occasionally, small children get lead poisoning from eating lead-based paint from the walls of old houses. Modern pipes are made of copper, and modern paint is lead-free, so new buildings are safe from the hazard of this toxic metal.

The air we breathe is no longer clean and pure. "Developments" that have made our lifestyle more comfortable (such as industrialization, urbanization and the use of private cars) all pollute the earth's atmosphere. Reducing air pollution should be a priority in all countries. Industries should invest in environmentally-friendly production methods. We should all use our cars less and buy vehicles that have catalytic converters and run on unleaded gasoline. Governments should legislate to reduce the levels of toxic emissions from cars, power stations, factories and domestic chimneys. Air pollution today is often invisible, but we should not ignore the danger it is causing to our own health, the health of our children and the health of the planet.

Exercises

Section A Summary writing

The following paragraph summarizes the answer to the question asked in the pre-reading exercise. Put one word only in each of the blank spaces to complete the paragraph.

<u>The main causes of air pollution</u>

A number of factors contribute to .... pollution. In particular the burning of brown .... gives off sulphur dioxide and soot, ... in certain weather conditions can cause .... In addition, industrial waste released high .... the atmosphere can produce sulphuric and .... acid, which are carried a long .... and cause acid rain. At ground .... there is also the problem of .... exhausts producing ozone and giving off ....

Section B Jumbled Words

Find the words from the chapter with the aid of the definitions.

1 to give off a gas TIME
2 to go down, to fall SEEDACRE
3 bad for you, damaging LURMFAH
4 poisonous COTIX
5 to join, come together BINCOME
6 things which pollute the air NATLOPLUTS
7 what water becomes when heated PARVO
8 another word for old DEERLYL

8 Water

Pre-reading
In a small group discuss the reasons why there is a shortage of water in the world nowadays and make a list of your reasons. Then compare your list with Table 1.

Table 1 *Causes of the world water shortage.*

Increase in water consumption Population growth Increase in per capita consumption
Pollution of water supplies Acid rain Industrial waste Sewage
Decrease in water reserves Dams Irrigation schemes Intensive farming Deforestation

One of the most urgent environmental problems in the world today is the shortage of clean water. Table 1 shows the causes of the water shortage. There are large differences in per capita water consumption between different countries. A comfortable lifestyle (with flush toilets, washing machines and public swimming pools) uses a lot of water. A lavish lifestyle (with automatic car-wash machines, Jacuzzis and backyard swimming pools) uses many times more. The average Kenyan uses five liters of water a day; the average American uses 1,000. More and more people in the world are adopting a Western lifestyle. So even if population growth stops, the water shortage will get worse.

Access to clean drinking water is a basic human right. But acid rain, industrial pollution and sewage dumping have made many sources of water undrinkable. Lakes, reservoirs and even entire seas have become vast pools of poison. Lake Baikal in Russia is one of the largest lakes in the world. It is also one of the most beautiful. The local people call it the Holy Sea. It contains a rich variety of animals and plants, including 1,300 rare species that do not exist anywhere else in the world. But they are being destroyed by the massive volumes of industrial effluent which pour into the lake every day. Until very recently, environmental standards in the former Soviet states were much lower than in the West. Even where laws existed, the government did not have the power to enforce them. Most industries simply ignored the regulations. In the past few years, **glasnost** has given people greater freedom of speech. They are now free to protest about the pollution. Some factories are now disposing of their waste more responsibly. But many others still pour untreated industrial waste into the Holy Sea.

The Mediterranean Sea occupies 1 percent of the world's water surface. But it is the dumping-ground for 50 percent of all marine pollution. Sixteen countries border on the Mediterranean. Almost all of them regularly dump shiploads of industrial waste a few miles off shore. Sewage effluents pour into the sea only meters from popular bathing beaches. In 1975, the United Nations Environment Program brought together these 16 countries and drew up the Mediterranean Action Plan. The countries agreed to stop dumping from ships and to reduce sewage pollution. Few, if any, of them have kept their word. In the 1950s, Japanese factories dumped waste containing mercury into the sea at Minamata Bay. Shellfish became contaminated with this very toxic heavy metal. Over 2,000 people developed brain damage and 40 of them died (Fig. 1). These tragic examples should teach us that the ocean is neither a garbage can nor a toilet.

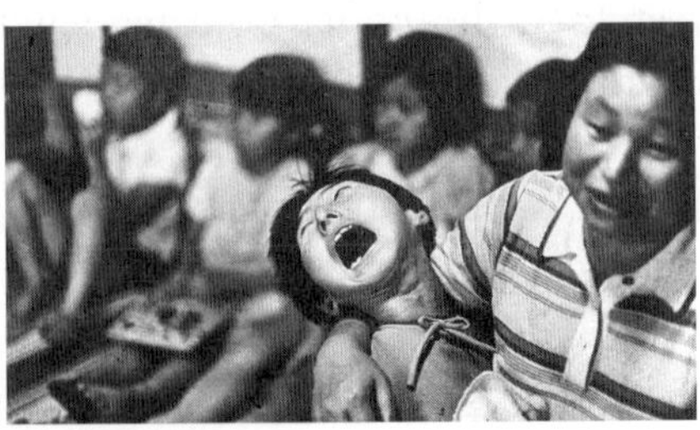

Figure 8.1 *Minamata disease.*

Sewage is a rich source of micronutrients, which are essential for the growth of plants and animals. Sewage sludge, and fertilizers washed off the land, increase the concentration of micronutrients (particularly nitrates) in the sea to dangerous levels. Plankton (tiny plants that float near the surface of the water) become so numerous that they cut out the light to deeper parts of the sea. This endangers plants that grow on the sea bed, which need the sun's light for photosynthesis. Seaweed is also very sensitive to changes in the level of micronutrients in coastal waters. One or two species of algae (seaweed) can outgrow all the other species. Overgrowth of algae can cause slimy, smelly, ugly deposits on beaches. Occasionally algae produce poisonous toxins that can kill fish or cause skin rashes in swimmers.

We condemn deliberate pollution of the water supply by industrial waste and sewage dumping. But we are usually impressed by "developments" such as huge dams, dikes and irrigation schemes. These are often magnificent feats of civil engineering. They cost a lot of money and use modern materials and equipment. We often assume that the people who plan and build these systems know what effect they will have on the environment. In fact, many dams and irrigation schemes have been environmental disasters. Three quarters of the world's water is used to irrigate crops, so inefficient or extravagant irrigation schemes can cripple a region's water supply. The Aral Sea in Russia was once the fourth-biggest lake in the world. It is now less than half the size it was in 1965. Badly-planned irrigation schemes have taken water from the rivers that fed the Aral Sea. In addition, overuse of pesticides on the cotton crops nearby has polluted the water with toxic chemicals. The damage to the Nile Valley caused by Egypt's Aswan Dam is described in Chapter 14. In some cases, major water diversion projects began because a new technology became available and governments wanted to demonstrate their new-found power over nature. Dams can also be a direct political tool. Rivers often flow through one country to get to another, so the first country can potentially control the flow of water into the second. Turkey has recently built several dams across the river Euphrates, and has already used these dams to restrict the water flowing through to Iraq and Syria. It has also signed an agreement to sell water to Israel.

"Development" projects can also make soil erosion worse. Forests and grasslands in a river valley soak up water after heavy rains and slowly release it back into streams and rivers. This prevents the valley from becoming dry and dusty in the months without rain. In addition vegetation also prevents erosion by holding the particles of soil together. If there is no vegetation, the soil crumbles away and is washed into the rivers as **silt**. Rivers become clogged with sediment. Lakes change from clear, blue pools into thick, muddy puddles. The destruction of rainforests, and intensive farming practices (such as heavy grazing of cattle and excessive plowing with powerful machines) both increase soil erosion. Because of deforestation and modern farming methods, the **sediment load** of the Yellow River in China is 1.6 billion metric tons per year, and that of the Ganges is 1.455 billion metric tons. The traditional farming methods used by **primitive** communities may seem inefficient, but the sediment loss from these methods is tiny.

The best things in life are free. But because water is free, we often take it for granted. A few years ago, people thought that the supply of clean water in the world was limitless. Today, many water supplies have been ruined by pollution and sewage. Others have dried up because we have diverted the water for hydroelectricity or badly-planned irrigation projects. The destruction of forests and grasslands has increased soil erosion. Clean water is now scarce, and we are at last beginning to respect this precious resource. Like other environmental resources, the clean water that remains is the property of our children and grandchildren. For their sake, we must fight to protect what is left of the water supply.

Exercises

Section A Summary writing

Using Table 1 write a paragraph summarizing the reasons why there is a shortage of water in the world.

<u>The reasons for the shortage of water in the world</u>

Factors affecting the demand for water and factors affecting the supply have meant that nowadays there is a shortage .... The demand has increased because .... as more and more countries have adopted a western lifestyle. As regards the supply of good quality water, this has been reduced by .... There is also less water available in reserves on account of ....

Section B

Read through the chapter. Then choose one of the statements in each question which corresponds to the meaning in the chapter.

1 a If the population falls, there will be enough water.
  b It is clear that the water shortage will get worse.
  c It is not really clear whether the water shortage will get worse.
  d If the population stops growing, there will be no water problem.

2 a Despite glasnost, there has been no improvement in treating industrial effluent in Russia.
  b Because of glasnost many factories now treat industrial effluent in Russia.
  c Very many people in Russia are protesting about industrial effluent, but very little is being done.
  d There has been some improvement in treating industrial effluent in Russia.

3 a The Mediterranean Action Plan has meant 16 countries reducing sewage pollution and dumping.

b The Mediterranean Action Plan has not had much success in reducing sewage pollution and dumping.
c The Mediterranean Action Plan has clearly had some success in reducing sewage pollution and dumping.
d The Mediterranean Action Plan couldn't possibly have been successful because of the big differences in the 16 countries.

4a The use of sewage sludge and fertilizers is bad for plants on the sea bed.
b It is good that sewage sludge and fertilizers help plankton to grow strongly.
c Sewage sludge and fertilizers do not really have a serious effect on the plants in the sea.
d Sewage sludge and fertilizers are especially bad for tiny plants like plankton near the surface of the water.

5a Polluting water with industrial waste and sewage is worse than the damage caused by poor civil engineering developments.
b The damage caused by poor civil engineering developments is worse than polluting water with industrial waste and sewage.
c People are starting to condemn poor civil engineering developments just as much as polluting water with industrial waste and sewage.
d People are less likely to condemn poor civil engineering developments than polluting water with industrial waste and sewage.

6a The Aral Sea is the fourth biggest lake in the world.
b The Aral Sea is polluted because of pesticides.
c The Aral Sea is smaller because rivers take the water away.
d The Aral Sea is smaller because irrigation schemes take water straight from it.

7a Forests and grasslands cannot absorb all the rainwater so it then flows into streams and rivers.
b Forests and grasslands prevent particles of soil from holding together.
c Forests and grasslands wash the soil into rivers as silt.
d Forests and grasslands are necessary to keep valleys supplied with water.

9 Soil

> *Pre-reading*
> What do you think have been the effects of using pesticides and artificial fertilizers in modern farming? Discuss this question in a small group and make a list of the effects. Then compare your discussion with the points raised by the author in paragraphs 3 and 4 of the chapter.

Soil forms over thousands of years from the **weathering** of rock. There are three types of weathering: physical weathering (where temperature changes cause the rock to expand and contract until it shatters into pieces), chemical weathering (where carbon dioxide and water form a weak acid that dissolves rocks such as limestone) and biological weathering (where the rock is broken down by the action of living things such as plant roots and bacteria). Fig. 1 shows the composition of a typical soil. The top layer of the soil (**topsoil**) is rich in **humus** — a dark, fibrous material formed from decaying organic matter. Humus contains micronutrients such as nitrogen (see below), minerals such as iron, and microorganisms that break down the organic matter. Humus absorbs moisture and binds the inorganic particles together. The quality (or fertility) of soil depends on the amount of humus in it — the organic content. Good quality topsoil is dark, moist and crumbly. The middle layer of the soil contains less organic material, but it is rich in minerals because these get washed down with the rain. The lower layer (**subsoil**) is made of inorganic material, similar to the parent rock which originally formed the soil.

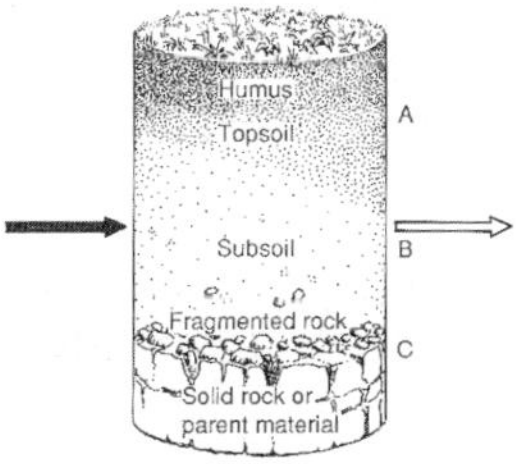

Figure 9.1 *Composition of a typical soil.*

All living things are made of protein, which contains **nitrogen**. Without nitrogen, plants and animals cannot grow, because they cannot build new tissue. Fig. 2 shows the **nitrogen cycle**. Traditional farming methods rotate cereal crops (which remove nitrogen from the soil) with leguminous plants (which replace the nitrogen). Intensive farming methods, where cereals are grown every year, tend to deplete the soil of nitrogen. Repeated cropping and overgrazing (that is, putting too many cattle on a small area of grassland) cause **erosion** of the top layers of the soil. The essential nitrates are removed with the topsoil so the nitrogen cycle, which is crucial to the balance of nature, is broken.

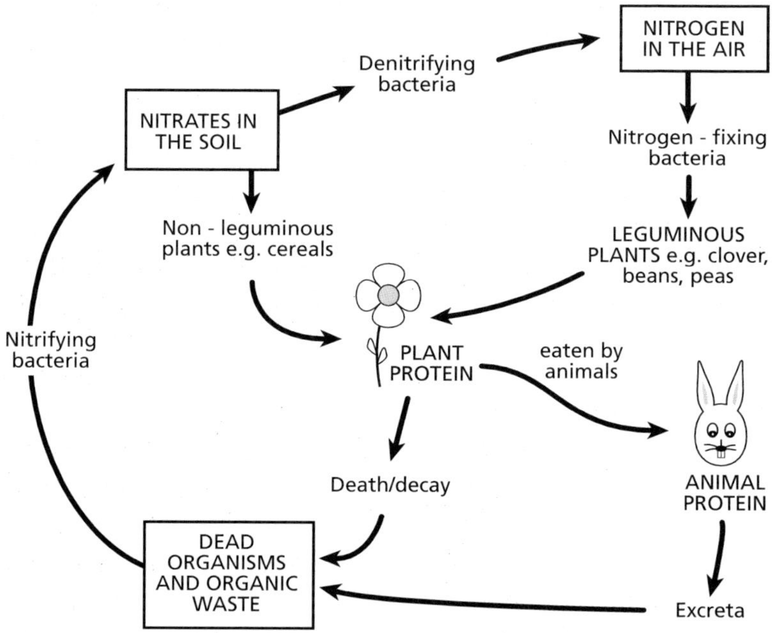

Figure 9.2 *The nitrogen cycle.*

The earth is losing 24 billion metric tons of topsoil every year through intensive farming methods and deforestation (see Chapter 3). The end stage of this loss of topsoil is **desertification**, where all the organic and mineral content of the soil has disappeared, leaving only poor quality subsoil, which cannot support plant growth. About 20 million hectares of productive land become barren every year because of soil erosion. Thirty percent of the world's land surface is threatened with desertification. Another hazard of intensive farming is **salinization**, which is caused by perennial irrigation (that is, irrigation year after year without a break) in arid climates. All soil contains some salt, which is washed away when it rains. Where rainfall is minimal, the salt content of the soil is very high. Evaporation from reservoirs and irrigation channels increases the salinity of the water. When a new irrigation scheme raises the water table, salt from the soil dissolves in the water and rises to the surface. Unless the area is left fallow and unirrigated for a season so that the salty water can drain away, the land will become permanently salinized and unable to support plant life.

The quality of soil can be improved by adding **fertilizers**. Organic fertilizers are made from animal and plant material such as **compost** (rotting plant matter) or **manure** (animal excreta) which return essential micronutrients such as nitrates, phosphates and potash to the soil. Artificial (inorganic) fertilizers are manufactured compounds that contain high concentrations of these micronutrients; they are much more powerful than natural organic fertilizers. But they cause environmental damage by a process called **eutrophication**. Excess nitrogen is washed out of the soil with the run-off after it rains. It passes into rivers and lakes, and encourages the growth of algae (seaweed) in the water and of wild plants on nearby land. Overgrowth of algae upsets the balance of nature in lakes and seas (see Chapter 8). Overcrowding on the banks causes the plants to rot and die. The air becomes contaminated with nitrous oxide which contributes to the greenhouse effect. Like nitrates, phosphates and potash are taken up by growing plants and returned to the soil in animal excreta. The phosphates and potash in artificial fertilizers must be extracted from rocks by mining, but these mineral resources will not last forever. If we continue to dump animal and human waste into the sea instead of using it to fertilize the soil, our entire reserves of these precious minerals will be lost at the bottom of the oceans. Artificial fertilizers add a few selected micronutrients, but because they cause rapid plant growth they deplete the soil of other nutrients. Plants grown in artificial fertilizers are often tasteless and have a low nutritional value. They may be contaminated with chemical residues from the fertilizer manufacturing process. For both environmental and health reasons, many consumers today prefer to buy **organic vegetables** — that is, vegetables grown without any artificial fertilizers.

Organic vegetables are also grown without **pesticides**. These chemicals kill insects and other pests but they are poisonous to many other living things as well — including man. Pesticides are absorbed by the crops and washed into the rivers and the sea. They often become concentrated by the **food chain**. Some pesticides accumulate in the human body and are secreted in breast milk. About 20,000 people in the world, including many children, die each year from accidentally drinking or inhaling pesticides. Some pesticides may cause cancer, miscarriage or even birth defects. The effect of pesticides on increasing crop yields is often transient. Some pests become resistant to the chemicals. The pesticides might destroy the pest's natural predators, so the farmer soon sees a paradoxical increase in the pest population. The so-called "miracle strains" of high-yield cereal crops are particularly vulnerable to pests. The farmer must use higher concentrations of pesticides each year to control the problem. Intensive farming of high-yield strains is usually associated with heavy use of both fertilizers and pesticides. Organic farming methods do not usually use these high-yield strains.

Intensive farming methods which successfully increase crop yields in temperate zones often fail in tropical climates. There are several reasons for this. First, tropical countries usually have poor soil. Tropical heat kills microorganisms, so tropical soil has a lower organic content. This reduces its capacity to absorb water and makes it particularly vulnerable to erosion. When rain comes in the tropics, it usually arrives in a huge deluge after several months of no rain at all. The sandy topsoil is easily washed away, leaving soil of even poorer quality beneath. Second, there are more pests. In temperate areas, the cold winter kills off many of the weeds, fungi, insects and other pests. In tropical zones, there is no cold season. The pests thrive in the constant heat and frequently cause failure of crops. They spread easily from one field to another, so they cause particular damage when a single crop is grown intensively on a vast area of land. In general, tropical regions are more suited to subsistence farming (where a variety of small-scale crops is grown) than to the large-scale, intensive production of cash crops. Third, livestock in the tropics is heavily infested with parasites — that is, small organisms such as tapeworms which live in the intestines of pigs and cattle. The parasites use up precious micronutrients and so the animals grow up small and weak. The yield from both arable and cattle farming in tropical regions is usually one-quarter to one-third that of temperate regions. If the people try to introduce intensive farming methods, yields may increase temporarily, but they eventually fall still further and soil erosion accelerates.

A handful of soil looks inert and uninteresting. But good quality, fertile soil contains all the basic building blocks of life. Beneath the thin layer of soil lies a planet as lifeless as the moon. Intensive farming techniques increase crop yield in the short term but deplete the quality of the soil in the long term, particularly in tropical regions. At best, crop yields fall and at worst, the soil becomes ecologically bankrupt and unable to sustain crops at all. Intensive farming is yet another example of the "live now, pay later" philosophy that may ultimately cost us the earth.

Exercises

Section A Complex sentences and summary writing

Below is a list of points made by the author on artificial fertilizers:

1 Artificial fertilizers cause environmental damage.
2 Too much nitrogen causes too much growth of seaweed and wild plants nearby.
3 The plants rot and die.
4 The air becomes contaminated with nitrous oxide.
5 This leads to the greenhouse effect.
6 The phosphates and potash in artificial fertilizers are mined.
7 The supply of minerals is limited.
8 Artificial fertilizers add a few micronutrients.
9 They also take out other micronutrients.
10 Plants are poor nutritionally.
11 Plants can be tasteless.

12 Plants are possibly harmful because of chemical residues.

i) Construct complex sentences in the way suggested:

1 Join sentences 1 and 2 with *because*.
2 Join sentences 3, 4 and 5 with *and* and *which*.
3 Join sentences 6 and 7 with *so*.
4 Join sentences 8 and 9 with *but*.
5 Join sentences 10, 11 and 12 with *and*.

ii) Now use the following words and phrases in the correct order to connect your complex sentences and make a paragraph which summarizes the effects of using fertilizers.

1 As regards the food grown,
2 Moreover,
3 Overall,
4 As a result,

iii) Finally, compare your version with the model in the Key to the Exercises.

Section B

Read through the chapter carefully. Then complete the following to form sentences according to the meaning of the chapter.

1 Plants and animals need nitrogen so that ....
....

2 The effect of repeated cropping and overgrazing on the soil is
....
....

3 Good quality soil contains ....
....

4 The amount of topsoil being lost every year because of deforestation and intensive farming ....
....

5 Desertification means that ....
....
....

6 Salinization occurs when ....
....

7 Organic fertilizers can be either ....
....

8 Pesticides are chemicals which ....
....

9 High-yield strains are not usually ....
....

10 There are fewer pests in ....
....

11 Parasites are ....
....
....
....

12 Although intensive farming increases crop yield, ...
....
....

10 Food and famine (1): the land

Pre-reading

With your partner try to decide whether the following statements are true or false. Guess! Then see if you were right by quickly scanning the text.

1. The demand for food in the world has increased very much during the last 40 years.
2. In the last 10 years food productivity has risen.
3. There is still plenty of land available for cultivation.
4. World population is rising by 93 million every year.
5. In the next few years there will be enough food in the world.
6. A quarter of all children in developing countries are near to starvation.
7. A bigger demand for hamburgers in the 1970s and '80s has meant Third World farmers are producing feed for cattle.
8. Eating meat is sensible for people in all countries of the world.
9. The production of meat requires the same amount of land as the production of cereals or vegetables.
10. Two thirds of all the grain produced in the world is used to feed animals on farms.

Man has been growing crops for 10,000 years. Until about 1960, increased demand for food was met simply by using more land to grow crops. As the population grew, farmers extended the area of land that they cultivated. From 1960 to 1980, increased demand for food was met mainly by increasing the productivity of the land. Farmers used techniques such as irrigation (which brings water to dry soil), terracing (which allows cultivation on steep hillsides — Fig. 1), and fallowing (where fields lie uncultivated on alternate years to replenish the soil) to grow crops on previously unproductive land. The 1960s and '70s were also the decades of so-called "miracle strains" of rice and other staple crops, which produced a much higher yield per hectare. The availability of cheap nitrogen fertilizer (see Chapter 9) also helped to increase productivity between 1960 and 1980. Fifteen years ago, we were becoming complacent about our ability to feed the world's population. But over the past 10 years, food productivity has reached a plateau, and has even begun to fall. There is little new land available for cultivation. High-yield strains of rice and cereals have already replaced standard strains in most places. The promise of even more efficient strains through genetic engineering has not yet been fulfilled, and scientists are increasingly pessimistic about whether further improvements are possible. In some cases, increases in productivity have been a false economy. Continuous cropping of cereals reduces the quality of the soil and increases soil erosion. As Chapter 9 explained, the world is losing millions of tons of topsoil every year through intensive farming methods. The productivity of these exhausted soils will soon begin to fall.

Figure 10.1 *Terracing enables cultivation of land on steep mountainsides.*

A crisis is looming. Over the past 40 years, world demand for food has tripled. World population is still rising at a rate of 93 million people every year. But food production cannot increase indefinitely. Per capita grain production reached a peak in 1985 and is now declining. In 1987, world reserves of grain were sufficient to last for 101 days; by 1989 they would only last 54 days. The "grain mountains" of surplus cereals produced by high-technology farming in Western Europe will be a short-lived phenomenon. In the next few years, demand for food will exceed supply. Many countries in the world are already desperately short of food. For years, countries such as Sudan and Ethiopia have fluctuated between meager subsistence and overt famine. Three factors can push a country into famine: drought, civil war and pestilence (such as a plague of locusts). But these things are not the causes of the food shortage, since they cause famine only when food reserves are already at a critically low level. Children with severe malnutrition — the starvation diseases marasmus and kwashiorkor — are uncommon even in the poorest countries. But mild nutritional deficiency is very common. A quarter of all children in the developing world suffer from mild to moderate malnutrition. Fifty to seventy percent have mild vitamin B deficiency. These children are teetering on the edge of starvation.

The food shortage in the Third World has been aggravated by the change in land use from subsistence farming to the production of cash crops for export. A few entrepreneurs take over large areas of land and drive the small peasant farmers out of business. Money comes into the country, but it does not create wealth for the people who need it. It goes into the pockets of a few business people. In an export-led Third World economy, the rich usually get richer while the poor get closer to starvation. The rich nations' love of meat has led directly to malnutrition and environmental damage in the Third World. In the 1970s and '80s, the demand for cheap beef increased as the U.S. hamburger industry grew. Many Third World farmers started producing cattle feed instead of grain for human consumption. In the poorest countries of the world, where the local population could barely get enough to eat, valuable farmland was used to fatten cows for export. (A further tragic consequence of the demand for cheap beef was the destruction of rainforests, described in Chapter 3.) In most countries, eating dead animals is a symbol of a civilized and sophisticated lifestyle. People in rich countries eat meat two or three times a day, and many people in poor countries wish they could do the same. Meat is considered a "quality" food. But in reality it is an inefficient way to feed the population. Animals only convert one-tenth of what they eat into protein, so the production of meat requires much more land than the production of cereals, soya beans or other vegetables for human consumption. Two-thirds of all the grain produced in the world goes to feed livestock. A change in people's attitude to food, so that meat ceases to be a status symbol, could reduce meat consumption significantly. Millions of hectares of land would be freed for more productive use.

Western countries, which have contributed greatly to the food shortage in the Third World, like to offer "food aid" to the poorer countries. They send huge quantities of grain to countries where there is overt or imminent famine. But food aid sometimes brings more problems than it solves. Distributing the food, and converting it to a form that can be eaten, can pose major problems. The surplus of wheat flour in Europe and North America is no use to a country devastated by famine and civil war. The people do not have the transportation system to distribute the flour or the tools to make it into bread. Dried skimmed milk, which is a by-product of the butter industry, is a useful and nutritious food. But it must first be mixed with vegetable oil to make a balanced meal, otherwise it will not be absorbed by undernourished children. In the past, sacks of dried skimmed milk dumped at the frontier of a starving country have become as hard as concrete while waiting for supplies of oil to mix with the milk. Badly-planned food aid programs are a waste of time and resources. There is another reason why food aid is becoming unpopular. It is, at best, a short-term strategy for dealing with an emergency. It can stifle the initiative of the local people and create a culture of dependency. It does nothing to solve the long-term shortage of food.

There are no easy solutions to the world food crisis. But three strategies will help to ease the problem. First, population growth must be controlled (see Chapter 2). Second, the short-term economic gains of intensive farming must be sacrificed and replaced with conservation-oriented methods that replenish the soil and improve long-term productivity. Third, we must encourage the people in developing countries to become self-sufficient in food production. This will be difficult because the economies of these countries are now heavily dependent on their cash crops. Business people will say that changing back to small-scale subsistence farming will be a step backward. Consumers in the rich countries, who now enjoy the luxury of cheap cash crops from the Third World, may protest. But if we care about feeding the world's poor, we must be prepared to change our own greedy lifestyles rather than simply dumping our surplus food on populations who cannot use it.

Exercises

Section A Summary Writing

The final paragraph summarizes the essential points of this chapter. This paragraph is given below with some blanks. Replace the blanks with a suitable preposition and write out the paragraph. Finally check your answers with the text.

There are no easy solutions .... the world food crisis, but three strategies will help to ease the problem. First, population must be controlled. Second, the short-term economic gains .... intensive farming must be sacrificed and replaced .... conservation-oriented methods that replenish the soil and improve long-term productivity. Third, we must encourage the people .... developing countries to become self-sufficient .... food production. This will be difficult because the economies .... these countries are now heavily dependent .... their cash crops. Business people will say that changing back .... small-scale subsistence farming will be a step backward. Consumers .... the rich countries, who now enjoy the luxury .... cheap cash crops from Third World, may protest. If, however, we care .... feeding the world's poor, we must be prepared to change our own greedy lifestyle rather than simply dumping our surplus food .... populations who cannot use it.

Section B Discussion Work

How do you feel about eating meat? Organize a class debate on the subject with two speakers *for* the motion and two speakers *against* it. The title of the motion could be that "people should stop eating meat."

11 Food and famine (2): the sea

Pre-reading

With your partner, consider the following two questions before looking at the chapter and in each question select one statement which you think is the correct answer. Then quickly scan the text to see if you were right.

1 Water covers
a 1/3 of the world's surface.
b 1/2 of the world's surface.
c 3/4 of the world's surface.
d 2/3 of the world's surface.

2 Nowadays the area where a country can fish in the water around that country is
a 370 kilometers.
b 70 kilometers.
c 170 kilometers.
d 17 kilometers.

Chapters 9 and 10 described the environmental problems caused by intensive farming and the cultivation of cash crops. Another example of environmental damage caused by man's hunt for food is the impact of the modern fishing industry. For thousands of years, fish have been an important part of the human diet. Almost all societies have developed techniques for catching fish. Small-scale fishing does no environmental harm. But from the mid-19th century, the industrialized nations have been using progressively bigger ships, finer nets and other more efficient methods of trapping fish. The stocks of fish cannot be replenished fast enough. Fishing is now big business. Most of the world's fishing industry is controlled by large corporations who compete fiercely with one another. They put profit before environmental responsibility. Almost every species of marine animal, from tiny anchovies to great whales (Fig. 1), is now only a small fraction of its former population.

Figure 11.1 *The whale — an endangered species.*

Until quite recently, the fishing zone around a country (that is, the area where fishing is restricted to boats from that country) was only a few kilometers wide. Political disputes over fishing rights were common, and countries even went to war over the so-called "freedom of the seas." The official limit for the fishing zones around countries is now 370 kilometers. In theory, each country is responsible for conserving the stocks of fish within this zone. But in reality, governments are reluctant to pass laws restricting the activities of their national fishing industries, when other countries continue to fish unrestricted in nearby waters. Some governments actually encourage the problem by subsidizing their own fishing industries. If they do this, even uneconomic fleets continue to do damage. In recent years, developing countries have begun to join in the depletion of the seas. Building large, mechanized fishing boats is a relatively low-technology process. In the 1960s, '70s and '80s, many growing economies in the Third World invested in the fishing industry. Banks and development agencies were keen to lend them money. Fish became a "cash crop" rather than a subsistence food. Large-scale deep-sea fishing for export depleted the catches of coastal communities who traditionally depended on fishing for their livelihood. A few powerful entrepreneurs profited while communities lost their main source of food and income.

In addition to problems close to the shore, there is a lucrative fishing industry, particularly for tuna, in the deep seas beyond national fishing zone boundaries. Huge fleets of ships come to an area of ocean, take all the available fish, and then move on to another area. Governments of individual countries are powerless to stop them. Some fishermen in Korea, Japan and Taiwan still carry out **drift netting** — that is, dragging huge nets (up to 50 kilometers long) between trawlers (Fig. 2). These nets trap and kill many animals, such as dolphins and turtles, which are of no interest to the fishermen. In 1989 the United Nations General Assembly adopted a resolution which banned drift netting in the high seas from 1992. But this, like many international laws and agreements, was easier to sign than it is to enforce. Another problem on the high seas is the hunting of whales. Whale hunting was banned by international agreement from 1986 to 1992 because whales were an endangered species and the method of killing was inhumane. Under pressure from Japan, Norway, Iceland and Denmark, the International Whaling Commission partially lifted the ban in 1992. Each country may now kill a certain quota of whales every year. The international campaign to "save the whales" (by reinstating the ban on whaling and punishing people who kill whales illegally) continues.

Figure 11.2 *Drift netting for tuna.*

Two-thirds of the world's surface is water. Most of this water does not belong to any particular country. Perhaps this is why so many nations plunder the oceans so selfishly. The world's oceans are so vast that it is almost impossible to believe that mankind has driven many marine species to the brink of extinction. But despite this fact, the seas hold great hope for the future. Whereas the earth's land surface has reached the limit of its productivity, the oceans can potentially provide large quantities of food for the world's ever-increasing population. Just as the production of beef cattle is an inefficient use of farmland, the production of large fish is an inefficient use of the seas. But aquatic plants such as seaweed and plankton have a high nutritional value and (because they are lower down the food chain) are relatively cheap to produce. Farming the oceans — that is, the deliberate cultivation of nutritious aquatic plants — is a new and exciting branch of food science. But the large-scale use of communal waters for this purpose will require careful planning and international co-operation, so that food production is both efficient and sustainable. It will also require a change in diet for most people in the world. A plateful of seaweed is a delicacy in Japan, but most people in the United States and Europe find such food unpalatable. Instead of exhausting the seas further in the hunt for traditional Western seafood such as cod, haddock and tuna, perhaps the Western nations' first priority should be to become more imaginative in their eating habits.

Exercises

Section A Parallel or Group Reading

i) Depending on the size of the class, either
   a) divide the class into two groups, so that one group reads the first two paragraphs and the other group reads the second two paragraphs.

or:

   b) divide the class into four groups so that each one reads a different paragraph.

ii) After reading the paragraph or paragraphs individually, the groups discuss and work out the main points of what they have read. Then they tell the rest of the class what their part of the chapter was about.

Section B Summary Writing

The following four sentences summarize the four paragraphs of the chapter. First of all, match each sentence with the appropriate paragraph. Then write out the four sentences in the correct order so that they form a paragraph summarizing the chapter.

1 With fishing zones recently increased to 370 kilometers, both industrialized and developing countries have been depleting the seas.

2 The seas have, however, great possibilities as regards cultivating aquatic plants for food, all of which will require careful international planning as well as a change in people's diet.

3 Nowadays fishing has become big business throughout the world and as a result stocks of fish have become much less than they were.

4 Beyond the fishing zones there is also profitable fishing and unfortunately whale hunting and drift netting still exist.

Section C

i) Find some words in the chapter ending in *tion* using these definitions.

1 a large business, a company c _ _ _ _ _ _ tion
2 a small part f _ _ _ tion
3 growing plants or crops c _ _ _ _ _ _ tion
4 reducing the quantity of something d _ _ _ _ tion
5 a decision r _ _ _ _ _ tion
6 the dying out of a species e _ _ _ _ _ tion
7 helping each other c _ _ _ _ _ _ tion
8 what is made or grown p _ _ _ _ _ tion

ii) Find some adjectives in the chapter ending in *al* using these definitions.

1 between different countries i _ _ _ _ _ _ _ _ _ _ al
2 something used by everyone c _ _ _ _ _ al
3 food which is good for you n _ _ _ _ _ _ _ _ al
4 existing nearby l _ _ al
5 legal or stated in rules o _ _ _ _ _ al
6 just concerned with one country n _ _ _ _ _ al
7 the land alongside the sea c _ _ _ _ al
8 just concerned with one person i _ _ _ _ _ _ _ al

12 Non-renewable energy resources: the fossil fuels

Pre-reading

1 Renewable sources of energy means that the source can be used forever to create the energy; non-renewable means that the source is limited and that one day it will come to an end. Consider the following types of energy and with your partner decide whether they are renewable or non-renewable.

a wind power
b water power
c gas
d coal
e solar power (from the sun)
f oil

Check your answers with the opening paragraph, which mentions the non-renewable sources.

2 What are the main forms of energy that are used in your country? Are the types of energy used changing at all? If so, why are they changing? Consider these questions with the rest of the class.

Fossil fuels are sources of energy that are buried under the ground: coal, oil and natural gas. They were all once living plant or animal material. Plants get their energy from the sun via photosynthesis:

carbon dioxide + water + light energy ———> carbohydrates + oxygen

The energy is stored in the bonds between carbon molecules in carbohydrates. When a fossil fuel is burned, the equation is reversed:

carbohydrates + oxygen ———> carbon dioxide + water + heat energy + light energy

The amount of energy in any fossil fuel depends on the carbon content—that is, the amount of carbon that it contains. All fossil fuels produce carbon dioxide, the most important greenhouse gas, when they burn.

Coal was formed about 300 million years ago. Trees and plants fell into swamps and decomposed into peat. Later, the peat became buried and compressed into coal. After many years, the coal formed black or brown layers within sedimentary rocks. These layers of coal are called seams. Hard, black coal (anthracite) has a high carbon content. We use this coal in our homes for domestic fires. Soft, brown coal (lignite) has a lower carbon content. It is used in power stations. All coal, but particularly brown coal, contains impurities; when the coal burns, sulphur dioxide and nitrogen oxides are produced from these impurities. If we heat coal in the absence of air, we make coke. Coke is a smokeless fuel that is used in the production of iron and steel. Today, coal provides 25 percent of world energy. It is particularly important in generating electricity. By-products of coal include plastics, paint, man-made fibers (such as nylon), pesticides and fertilizers. The known resources of coal in the world probably can provide about 400 billion metric tons. These reserves will last between 100 and 300 years if consumption does not change.

Oil was formed about 400 million years ago. Animals and plants that lived in the sea died and were buried under the sea bed. Their bodies decomposed and became compressed by the weight of the sea above them. Gradually, they became buried under rocks. Over thousands of years, the decomposed animal and plant material turned into crude oil. Oil accumulates in porous sedimentary rocks such as sandstone. Non-porous rocks, such as clay, do not let oil through. Oil is usually found about 2,000 meters below ground in a layer of porous rock that lies between two layers of non-porous rock. This is called a trap. A trap usually occurs when the layers of rock form an arch or anticline (Fig. 1). The buried oil is often under high pressure. If we drill through the upper layers of rock, the oil usually rises up to the surface under its own pressure. Oil has a high carbon content so it is a good source of energy. It is easier to reclaim and transport than coal. It is very important in the petrochemicals industry, which produces detergents, plastics, fertilizers, man-made fibers, cosmetics and industrial chemicals such as sulphuric acid. The discovery of large reserves of oil in the 1970s created wealth for the Middle Eastern countries, but led indirectly to the Third World debt (see Chapter 18). Today, oil provides 50 percent of world energy. But we have already used up 25 percent of the known oil reserves in the world. There are probably about 90 billion metric tons left. Fig. 2 shows the production and consumption of oil in 1985. If world oil consumption continues at the same rate, and if we do not discover new reserves of oil, we will run out of oil in about 2015.

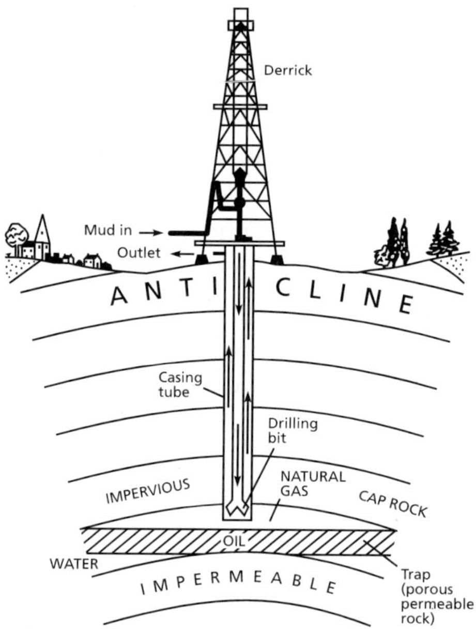

Figure 12.1 *Drilling for oil and natural gas.*

Natural gas (methane) often occurs with deposits of oil (Fig. 1). It has a very high carbon content. It comes out of the ground in a pure state so it does not need to be refined before use. It can travel long distances in underground pipes, and it is very clean to use. For all these reasons, natural gas is considered a high quality fuel. However, methane and its combustion product, carbon dioxide, are both greenhouse gases and contribute to global warming. Natural gas is used mainly in the home and in a few light industries. It provides about 20 percent of world energy today. World reserves of natural gas (about 60 billion metric tons) will probably last about 70 years.

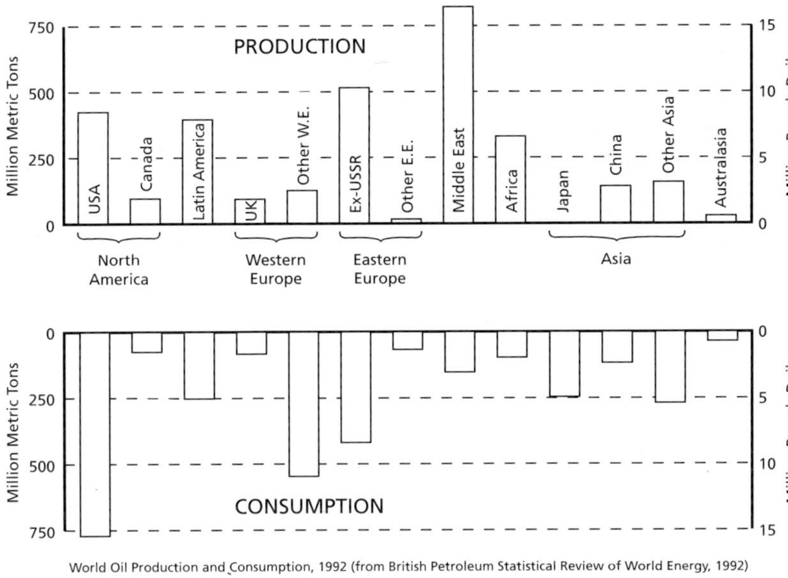

Figure 12.2 *World oil production and consumption 1985.*

The largest consumer of fossil fuels in the world is the electricity industry. People in rich countries have an almost unlimited supply of electricity. If we need light, heat or music, we just push a button. Electricity is so cheap that few of us think about the financial cost when we turn on an electrical appliance. But there is another cost — the cost to the environment. Every time you dry your hair, cook a meal or watch television, the greenhouse effect gets a little worse and a little more acid rain is generated. We should all try to use less electricity, for example by insulating our houses, turning off the light when we leave a room and using less hot water. Burning cheap, impure coal in an inefficient power station or primitive industrial process produces much more carbon dioxide than burning high quality coal in a modern, efficient system. Developed countries are beginning to introduce strict controls on industrial carbon dioxide emission. They can afford to buy the purest fuels and invest in the most efficient technology. Newly-industrializing countries, such as India and China, have large reserves of brown coal. They would like to use this coal as a cheap fuel for industrialization. But they cannot afford the sophisticated technology that would minimize carbon dioxide emission. Perhaps the developed countries, which have been responsible for most of the greenhouse effect in the past, should subsidize the transfer of technology to the newly-industrializing nations. This issue is discussed in Chapter 18.

Fossil fuels are running out. From the point of view of the environment, that is perhaps a good thing. But if we remain dependent on fossil fuels for most of our energy needs there will be a sudden crisis when the reserves are exhausted. We must try to develop alternative sources of energy before this crisis happens. One way of encouraging people to develop and use alternative energy is to make fossil fuels more expensive. In 1992, the countries of the European Community introduced an extra tax on fossil fuels — the carbon tax. Although the carbon tax is unpopular, most people agree that the price of a fuel should reflect its true cost — which should include the cost of damage to the environment. Some of the revenue from the carbon tax will pay for research into alternative sources of energy, which are discussed in Chapter 14.

Exercises

Section A Summary Writing

The concluding paragraph very much emphasizes the main point that fossil fuels are going to come to an end and suggests what should be done now for the future. Rewrite the paragraph by replacing the blanks either with the definite or indefinite article or putting in no article at all. Finally check your summary with the one in the chapter.

Fossil fuels are running out. From .... point of view of .... environment, that is perhaps .... good thing. If, however, we remain dependent on .... fossil fuels for most of our energy needs there will be .... sudden crisis when .... reserves are exhausted. We must try to develop .... alternative sources of .... energy before this crisis happens. One way of encouraging .... people to develop and use .... alternative energy is to make .... fossil fuels more expensive. In 1992, ... countries of .... European Community introduced .... extra tax on .... fossil fuels— .... carbon tax. Although .... carbon tax is unpopular, most people agree that .... price of .... fuel should reflect its true cost—which should include .... cost of damage to .... environment. Some of .... revenue from .... carbon tax will pay for .... research into .... alternative sources of .... energy.

Section B Word Puzzle

Down

1 With fossil fuels the energy is stored in .... (13 letters)

Across

1 To find out (8 letters).
2 .... eventually becomes coal when it is buried. (4 letters)
3 To produce, for example, electricity. (8 letters)
4 Money you have to pay back. (4 letters)
5 This means a liquid such as water can pass through. (6 letters)
6 Another word for natural gas. (7 letters)
7 You need this gas in order to live. (6 letters)
8 Little by little. (9 letters)
9 All coal contains this, but brown coal especially. (10 letters)
10 Where coal is found. (5 letters)
11 A by-product of coal. (8 letters)
12 Resources that can still be used. (8 letters)
13 Oil rises because of .... (8 letters)

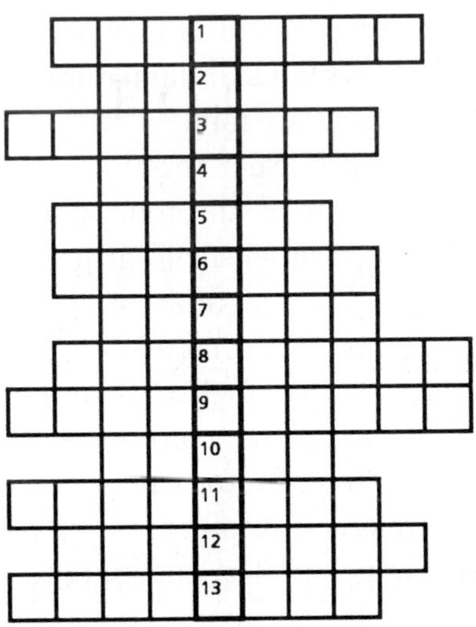

13 Nuclear power and nuclear waste

Pre-reading

1 In a small group, discuss what you think are the advantages and disadvantages of using nuclear power and say whether on balance you think it is a good source of power. Draw up a list of points for and against and then compare your points and opinions with what the author says.

2 Carry out a survey with the whole class and find out whether they are in favor of using nuclear power.

Nuclear (or atomic) energy comes from the energy stored within the nuclei of atoms, which are the basic building blocks of all matter. Atoms contain rings of tiny, negatively charged particles called electrons around a central core or nucleus. The nucleus contains positively charged particles (protons) and neutral particles (neutrons), held together by large amounts of energy. In all chemical reactions (such as the formation of salt — sodium chloride — from sodium and chlorine), the arrangement of the outer electrons changes but the nuclei of the sodium and chlorine atoms do not change. In a nuclear reaction, the arrangement of protons and neutrons in the nucleus changes. Most reactions in the natural world are chemical reactions. Nuclear reactions are rare.

There are two types of nuclear reaction: fission and fusion. In nuclear fission, the nucleus of an atom splits; some protons or neutrons escape, along with other small particles and a large amount of energy. For example, when an atom of uranium-235 splits, two smaller atoms ("fission fragments") are formed, and three neutrons are released. Uranium-235 is the fuel for the atomic bomb. In nuclear fusion, two nuclei join together; the protons and neutrons combine to form a larger nucleus. Some protons, neutrons and other particles escape, and energy is released. Another nuclear bomb, the hydrogen bomb, works on this principle. The energy produced from nuclear reactions is known as radiation; another name for the break-up of a nucleus is radioactive decay. Radiation is part of the electromagnetic spectrum. It causes darkening of photographic film; this principle is used in medicine to produce X-rays.

It is not easy to split the nucleus of an atom, or to fuse two nuclei together. So although there is a lot of energy stored in atoms, most it is of no practical use. This is a good thing. The world would not be very safe if atomic nuclei were always splitting and releasing energy! Most substances in the natural world are radiologically stable — that is, their nuclei do not spontaneously break up or combine with other nuclei. But some substances have unstable nuclei, which are continually breaking up. This natural radioactive decay does not normally release much energy because the nuclei break up very slowly, sometimes over hundreds of years. In the 19th century, the British physicist Baron Rutherford discovered how to split nuclei more quickly by firing high-speed neutrons at them. Neutrons released from the break-up of one nucleus bombard other nuclei, causing a chain reaction (Fig. 1) which leads to a sudden, explosive release of energy. This is the basis of both nuclear weapons and nuclear power, in which the energy of nuclear fission is converted to electricity.

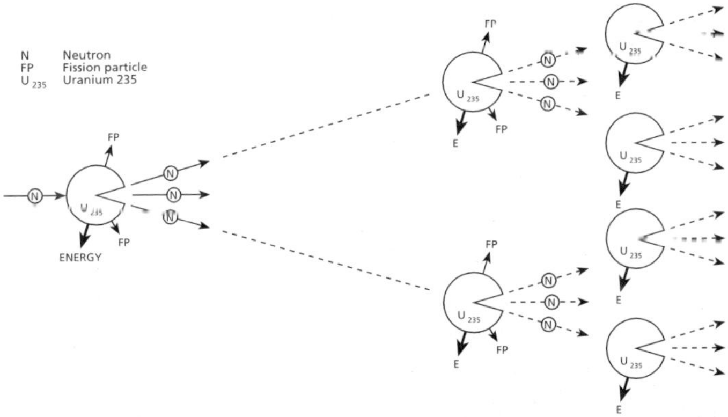

Figure 13.1 *Nuclear fission chain reaction.*

The most common type of nuclear power station today is the pressurized water reactor (Fig. 2). The fuel in the core of the reactor is uranium-235. The rate of breakdown of uranium-235 is carefully regulated using control rods made of heavy metal or graphite, which absorb free neutrons. The rods can be pushed into the radioactive core to stop the chain reaction. The energy from nuclear fission heats water under pressure to produce steam. This steam drives a turbine which generates electricity. Another source of water cools the core of the reactor when it becomes too hot. A more modern type of nuclear reactor is the fast breeder reactor. This reactor makes its own fuel by converting naturally-occurring uranium (uranium-238) to plutonium-239. The plutonium nuclei break down and release energy. The fast breeder produces more plutonium-239 than it can use to generate electricity, so the initial stock of plutonium increases or "breeds." Fast breeder reactors use uranium 50 times more efficiently than older style pressurized water reactors.

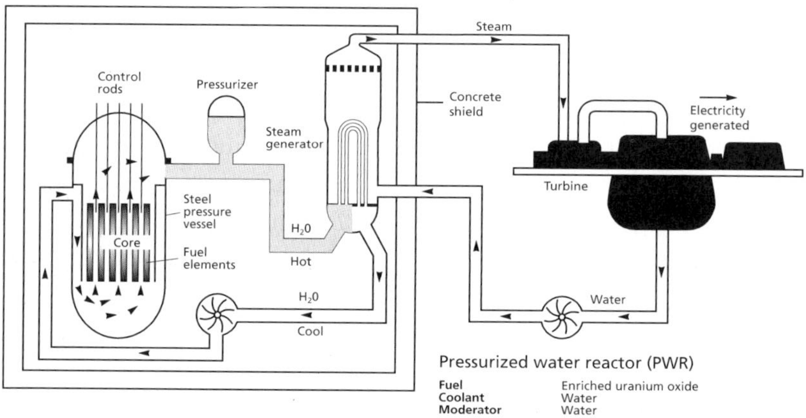

Figure 13.2 *Pressurized water reactor.*

There are several arguments for using nuclear power as a source of energy. First, the earth contains a limited supply of fossil fuels (see Chapter 12). Second, fossil fuels are very harmful to the environment. Nuclear power does not add to the greenhouse effect. Third, the earth contains a large supply of natural uranium. Nuclear power could, theoretically, supply all the world's energy needs for thousands (and possibly millions) of years. Fourth, nuclear power comes to the consumer as electricity, which is a clean and convenient form of energy. Although nuclear power stations are large and unattractive, they can be built long distances from population centers. Last, although the capital investment (that is, the initial cost of building the power station) is high, the cost of generating electricity from an established nuclear power station is relatively low.

However, there are many reasons why nuclear power is not the best source of energy. First, there is the danger of nuclear war. The pressurized water reactor works on the same principle as the atomic bomb — the fission of uranium-235. Thankfully, nuclear power has not been used for destructive purposes since World War II. But the widespread use of nuclear energy, and the development of new nuclear technology, increases the risk that nuclear weapons will be used again in the future. Plutonium-239 produced in fast breeder reactors is the raw material for modern thermonuclear warheads. Today's nuclear weapons are thousands of times more powerful than those used in 1945. The next nuclear war would probably destroy the world as we know it.

Second, even "peaceful" nuclear power is a danger to health. The radiation released when atoms split causes cancer and birth defects. Many survivors of the atomic bomb explosions in Hiroshima and Nagasaki later died of cancer, and women gave birth to deformed babies. Nuclear power stations are a potential source of this harmful radiation. If all goes well, the radiation stays within the core of the reactor and is absorbed by the control rods. But accidental leaks of radiation occur. The massive radiation leak from Chernobyl in the Soviet Union in 1986 was caused by a fire in the reactor. The radiation traveled thousands of miles, contaminating farmland and livestock. People living in or near Chernobyl developed cancers, particularly of the thyroid gland. Power stations built in the developed countries have safety features which would probably prevent a similar disaster in the West. But because the capital investment of building a nuclear power station is so high, newly-industrializing countries cannot always afford to include the best safety features.

Third, there are the problems of nuclear reprocessing and nuclear waste. Impurities build up within the core of a nuclear reactor and stop it working efficiently. The radioactive fuel must be reprocessed regularly. It is transported in a specially shielded container to a **reprocessing plant**, where the impurities are removed. These impurities are highly radioactive and dangerous to health. They must be stored deep underground in steel or concrete boxes. Eventually they will decay into stable elements, but this takes a long time. Plutonium-239, which is the most toxic man-made substance in the world, has a half-life of 24,000 years — that is, it takes 24,000 years to lose half its radioactivity. There is no easy or permanent method of disposing of radioactive waste. An accident at a reprocessing plant could be even more devastating than one at an ordinary nuclear power station.

A few years ago, many of us thought that nuclear power was the easy answer to the world's energy problems. It was, we thought, a clean, modern and efficient way to generate almost unlimited amounts of electricity. But today's nuclear power will be tomorrow's radioactive waste. We cannot make radioactive waste safe; we can only bury it and try to forget about it. It will be a problem for our children, our children's children and many generations after them. No wonder so many people today are wearing T-shirts and badges saying, "Nuclear power: no thanks."

Exercises

Section A Summary Writing

Listed below are points made by the author for and against nuclear power. Use them to write a summary by completing the framework provided. Write out your paragraph in full.

1 The supply of fossil fuels is limited.
2 Fossil fuels are harmful to the environment.
3 There is a large supply of uranium.
4 Nuclear power in the form of clean, efficient electricity could be used for at least thousands of years.
5 Ugly nuclear power stations can be located far from places where people live.
6 The cost of building a power station is high, but the cost of producing electricity is low.
7 There is a greater risk of a terrible nuclear war.
8 Nuclear accidents are possible with detrimental consequences for people's health and the environment.
9 Nuclear reprocessing is very dangerous to health.
10 Nuclear waste cannot really be made safe.
11 The disadvantages are greater than the advantages.

A number of arguments can be advanced in favor of .... Firstly, the supply of fossil fuels .... and in any case they.. .... Secondly, ... large supply of uranium, ... in the form of clean, efficient electricity .... for at least thousands of years. Thirdly, ugly nuclear power stations can be located far .... Moreover, although such stations are expensive ...., the cost of generating electricity .... There are, however, serious disadvantages to using .... The first point is that .... and nuclear accidents are also possible .... In addition, nuclear reprocessing .... to health .... cannot really be made safe. Therefore, on balance, the disadvantages ....

Section B Jumbled Words

Using the definitions, re-arrange the letters to find words used in the chapter.

1 negatively charged particles TELESNORC
2 a type of nuclear reaction NISFISO
3 escaping of a gas or radiation KALE
4 energy from nuclear reactions DARTINAIO
5 to free SEELEAR
6 to divide TIPLS
7 constant, not changing BEATLS
8 to change TONVERC
9 this is found in a nuclear power station CATRORE
10 the first, the one at the beginning NITILIA
11 the person who uses or buys something REMUSCON
12 working well FITIFCEEN
13 to find out SIDREVCO
14 to get away SECPEA
15 to happen ROCUC

14 Alternative energy

> *Pre-reading*
> With your partner, try to think of types of energy in nature which can be used again and again and write them down. Then compare your ideas with types discussed in the chapter by quickly scanning the text and glancing at the illustrations.

Energy comes in many forms — heat, light, sound, electrical and mechanical. There is no shortage of energy in the world. If you stand on the beach on a windy day you can see the strength of the wind and the waves, and the powerful burning light from the sun. The problem is how to convert this energy into the type of energy we need most today — electricity. A device that converts one form of energy to another is called a generator. The traditional generator converts heat energy from coal or gas into electrical energy. The generators of the future will harness renewable forms of energy in a similar way. **Wind power** has been used for hundreds of years in the form of the old-fashioned windmill, which converted one form of mechanical energy (wind) into another (the milling process). The modern version of the windmill is the aerogenerator (Fig. 1), which converts wind energy into electrical energy. The **aerogenerator** is relatively cheap and quick to build. It would take about two years to build a wind-powered electricity generating station, compared with 10 years for a power station based on fossil fuels. Wind power is clean and plentiful, and an aerogenerator does no damage to the environment. But aerogenerators are noisy, and the electricity cannot be stored easily for calm days. Wind power cannot, of course, be used in places where there is not much wind! Aerogenerators are best sited in coastal or mountainous areas. The Aran Islands are three tiny islands off the coast of Ireland that supply all their own energy needs from aerogenerators.

Figure 14.1 *Aerogenerators.*

Water can provide power in three ways: wave, tidal and hydroelectric. Fig. 2 shows two devices for harnessing **wave power** — Cockerell's rafts and Salter's ducks. These devices are not very efficient; they convert only 1–5 percent of the wave energy to electricity. But this does not matter much, because the wave energy is plentiful. The biggest technical problem is transmitting the electrical energy from the sea to the land. Wave power stations can potentially upset the local ecosystem. They must be carefully planned and sited where they will do little damage to marine and shore life. **Tidal energy** is harnessed by building a **barrage** across a river estuary with a large tidal range — that is, a large difference between high tide and low tide. Power is generated either intermittently (when water flowing back out to sea on the ebb tide is used to drive turbines), or continuously (when the energy of the rising tide is also used). However, there are very few suitable sites for tidal power stations. The only working barrage today is on the Rance Estuary in France, but several countries are planning to construct similar systems.

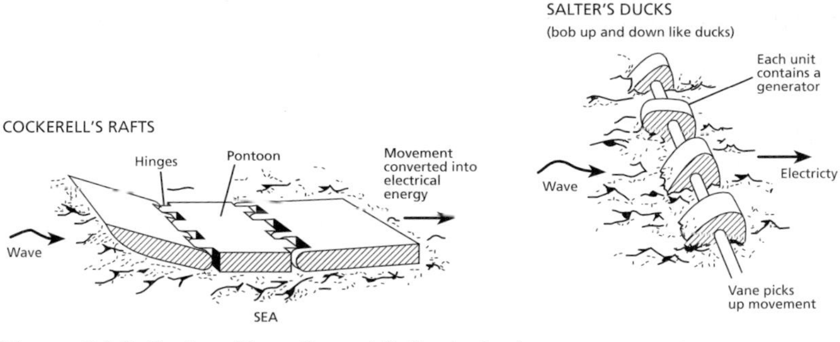

Figure 14.2 *Cockerell's rafts and Salter's ducks.*

Hydroelectric energy uses the mechanical energy from flowing rivers to generate electricity. It needs fast-flowing water, so hydroelectric power stations are usually sited in mountainous regions and where the current of the river is fast. The current is much lower in the dry season, so most hydroelectric projects include reservoirs and dams to store water. Electricity can then be generated all year round. Some hydroelectric stations pump water back to a high reservoir during the night (when demand for electricity is low). Like wave and tidal power, hydroelectric power has a high capital cost but low running costs. In Norway, which has many suitable mountain rivers, 90 percent of the country's energy comes from hydroelectricity. Hydroelectric power is a clean and renewable source of energy, and can be environmentally friendly. For example, there are about 80,000 small-scale hydroelectric turbines in China, which provide electricity to one-third of Chinese towns. However, large-scale hydroelectric projects are usually *not* environmentally friendly. Dams and reservoirs can destroy the ecological balance of the rivers and surrounding wetlands. Local people, who are a part of this ecosystem, can lose their homes and their livelihood. For example, the Aswan Dam in Egypt was built across Lake Nasser as part of a huge hydroelectric project. The dam caused many unforeseen environmental problems. Most of the lake's natural animal and plant life died. Water-borne diseases such as malaria and schistosomiasis increased. The Nile, which had been a wide, beautiful blue river, became no more than a trickle of water in some places. The land in the Nile Valley has become dry and unproductive. People whose families farmed this land for thousands of years must now leave in search of a more fertile place to live. They are "development refugees."

Solar power is energy generated from the sun. Many electronic devices, such as watches and calculators, can use the sun's energy directly to provide the power they need. Light energy from the sun changes the electrical conducting properties of the silicon crystals, and a tiny electric current starts to flow. This system is called a **solar cell**. Although solar cells used on earth do not provide much power, satellites in space run on the same principle. They get many times more energy because they are closer to the sun. In the future, workers in space may build huge power stations from solar cells many kilometers wide. The electricity generated could be beamed down to earth as microwaves and then converted back into electricity. Most of the solar power that we use today is based on a much simpler principle than the silicon solar cell. Solar panels on the roofs of houses heat water directly for bathing and central heating systems. The industrial version of the solar panel is the **solar furnace**, in which huge, curved solar panels, together with a system of mirrors, concentrate a large amount of solar energy onto a small area. The heat energy makes steam for generating electricity. Solar power is clean, renewable, non-polluting and does not damage the environment. It is potentially one of the most important sources of energy in the world. A major disadvantage of solar energy is that the amount of energy generated depends on the season, the part of the world and the weather on a particular day. Another disadvantage is that the raw materials for solar panels, such as glass and aluminum, are quite expensive.

Geothermal energy is energy from the hot center of the earth. The earth has a core of molten rock beneath its solid outer crust. This crust is usually between one and 50 kilometers thick. But in some places (such as Iceland and New Zealand) it is very thin; the hot molten rock is only a few meters beneath the surface. Energy from this molten rock is already widely used to heat homes and swimming pools in New Zealand, and in a few places it is used to generate electricity. If we developed the technology to bore deeper beneath the earth's surface, many other countries could use geothermal energy. Because there is so much molten rock within the earth, the potential supply of geothermal energy is almost limitless.

The natural world contains many sources of energy. It is possible to convert the energy of the wind, the sea, the rivers, the sun and the hot center of the earth into useful electrical energy. But because alternative energy is a young science, the generators that do this are relatively primitive and inefficient. We need more research into alternative energy. Environmentally-conscious governments must give more funds to research scientists so that they can develop more efficient ways of harnessing natural energy sources.

Exercises

Section A

Read through the chapter and answer the following questions using sentences.

1 What type of energy do people need most?
2 Where is the best place to put aerogenerators?
3 How can a generator be defined?
4 What are the advantages of wind power?
5 How many forms of water power are there and what are they?
6 What is the biggest difficulty with wave power?
7 Why must wave power stations be carefully planned and located?
8 What is the biggest drawback of tidal power?
9 How can electricity be generated all the year round in hydroelectric power stations?
10 In what ways are hydroelectric, wave and tidal power similar?

Section B Summary writing

i) Which paragraph do you think best summarizes the chapter? Discuss this question with your partner.

ii) The final paragraph best summarizes the essentials of the chapter. This paragraph is reproduced below with a number of blank spaces. Write out the paragraph, putting one word in each of the blank spaces. Finally, check your version with the text.

The natural world contains many [1] .... of energy. It is possible to [2] .... the energy of the wind, the [3] ...., the rivers, the sun and the [4] .... center of the earth into useful [5] .... energy. However, because alternative energy is [6] .... young science, the generators do [7] .... are relatively primitive and inefficient. We need [8] .... research into alternative energy. Environmentally-conscious governments [9] .... give more funds to research scientists [10] .... that they can develop more efficient [11] .... of harnessing natural energy sources.

15 Urban expansion

Pre-reading
Talk about the following two questions with your partner.

1 Where do you think towns and cities are growing the most nowadays?
2 What were towns and cities like in Britain in the nineteenth century as a result of the industrial revolution?

Then quickly scan the opening paragraph and the rest of the chapter to compare your ideas with the author's.

In the year 1800, 20 percent of the British population lived in towns or cities; by 1900, the proportion had increased to 80 percent. The cause of the increase was the **industrial revolution**. New labor-saving machinery put many rural farm workers out of work while the growth of factories created jobs in the towns. Urbanization started with a factory, built close to the source of raw materials such as coal and iron. Roads and railroads grew out from the industrial centers. Houses were built close to the factories, on any suitable piece of land. The science of town planning did not yet exist, and the result was often an ugly and unhealthy **urban sprawl**, with no open spaces, not enough schools or hospitals, and inadequate amenities (such as clean water and sewage services). The quality of life was poor. Diseases of poverty and overcrowding, particularly tuberculosis, cholera and typhoid, were very common. By the end of the 19th century, the British people had learned that they should plan the growth of towns and cities. In 1899 the British town planner Ebenezer Howard designed a new town, Welwyn Garden City, which had wide tree-lined streets, separate industrial and residential areas, several large parks and open spaces, and carefully planned schools and hospitals (Fig. 1).

Figure 15.1 *Welwyn Garden City.*

The industrial revolution has now reached almost every country in the world. But unlike 19th century Britain, most developing countries today do not have healthy, growing economies. Modern labor-saving machinery, and — perhaps more significantly — the concentration of land ownership into the hands of a rich elite, is making rural workers redundant. They migrate to the towns to look for work. But often, there is no work for them in the towns either. As well as the problems of rapid population expansion, spreading urban slums and inadequate sanitation, many Third World cities also have the problem of mass unemployment. Even when there are no jobs available, people still flock to the cities. Some seek bright lights and excitement, or a better education for their children. But some just want to stay alive. A person who has no home and owns no land has a better chance of survival in a large city than in a rural area.

Urban expansion in the Third World today is a more complex phenomenon than the growth of towns in 19th century Britain. **Economic migration** (that is, coming to the towns in search of work), is only one problem. Another is **indigenous population growth** (that is, when the people who already live in a city have more children) and a third problem is the deteriorating state of the environment. In some developing countries, women walk for many hours every day to fetch wood for fuel. Because the forests are getting smaller, they must walk farther each day. When the forests are more than a day's journey away, the family must move to a new part of the country closer to the forest. Many families now move to the large towns and cities instead. They give up subsistence farming and hope that the man will find a job in a factory or a shop. About 30,000 people go to Delhi every month because the land will no longer support them, usually because it has run out of fuel. These people are known as **environmental refugees**. The population of Mexico City is already 22 million. Through a combination of economic migration, indigenous growth and environmental refugees, it is increasing by half a million people every year. Bombay is growing by 300,000 people a year. In comparison, the population of New York has been stable at 15 million for two decades.

Each year, the sprawl of urban slums on the outskirts of many Third World cities gets wider and life gets harder for the inhabitants (Fig. 2). New migrants build more houses from cardboard, corrugated iron, wood, plastic and anything else they can find. Some people simply live in tents. The water and sewage services cannot grow fast enough. Neither can health services, transportation systems or waste disposal services. In Bangkok, one-third of the population has no access to clean water, and only 2 percent of the population is connected to the sewage system; a quarter of the city's garbage is dumped on waste ground or thrown into rivers and canals. Diseases of poverty and overcrowding, which are now rare in developed countries, are major killers in the urban slums of the Third World. Other health hazards are industrial pollution from factories sited in the middle of large residential areas, and traffic congestion in narrow streets which were not designed for motor vehicles. In addition, there are social problems. When there is no legal way of making a living, people turn to stealing, violent crime, drugs and prostitution. The poorest cities in the world are also the most dangerous.

Figure 15.2 *Mexico City.*

Everyone in a city needs food and shelter, and everyone produces waste. People travel out from the city to look for food, fuel and building materials and to dump their waste. The longer a person has lived in a city, the less he or she will respect the rural environment. Unemployed and destitute slum-dwellers cut down the forests and bleed the soil of its nutrients in their fight for survival. Rivers and lakes become polluted with industrial effluent and sewage. Many cities in the developing world are now surrounded by a wide band of desert where nothing can grow and where the water is undrinkable.

In 1990, 25 percent of the population of the developing world lived in large towns or cities. By 2025 the proportion will be 46 percent. Town planning in many developing countries is often a futile exercise. Urban expansion is occurring so fast, and the governments of these countries have so little money, that it is simply not possible to provide safe housing and basic amenities for everyone. Some governments have tried desperate measures like busing people back to their villages or driving bulldozers through shanty towns. These short-sighted policies will not solve the problem. Like most major environmental issues, the problem of urban expansion in the Third World has no simple solution. It will be helped by many of the measures discussed in other chapters in this book: population control, preservation of the rainforests, conservation of energy and resources, control of industrial pollution, improved public transport systems, and recycling of waste. Above all, we must address the issue of poverty, which underlies almost all other problems in the developing world (see Chapter 18).

Exercises

Summary Writing

Answer the following questions by using the words of the question exactly and in full, and also by referring to the chapter.

Example: Is population growing very much in Third World cities nowadays?

Answer: Population is growing very much in Third World cities nowadays.

1. Are there three main reasons for this urban expansion?
2. Are these reasons related to economic migration, indigenous population growth and environmental refugees?
3. Can the various services of water, sewage, health, waste disposal and transport cope at all with the ever-increasing numbers?
4. Is one of the consequences of this the existence of diseases associated with poverty?
5. What are other health hazards?
6. Are there social problems of crime, drugs and prostitution?
7. Can people make a living legally?

Write out your sentences to make one paragraph, also using the example given.

a Join sentences 1 and 2 with *which*.
b Begin sentence 3 with *however*.
c Join sentences 6 and 7 using *because* and begin the new sentence with *moreover*.
d Give your paragraph a title.

16 Industrial pollution and waste disposal

Pre-reading

Which of the following industries do you think causes the most industrial air pollution?

a chemicals
b steel
c electricity
d textiles
e gas

Talk to your partner. Guess if you do not know! Then quickly glance through the opening paragraph to check your answer.

The volume of both industrial and domestic waste has increased dramatically over the past 50 years. Industrial air pollution includes the greenhouse gases **carbon dioxide** and **chlorofluorocarbons** (see Chapter 6). It also includes **sulphur dioxide** and **nitrogen oxides**, which lead to acid rain. The largest single cause of industrial air pollution is the electricity industry. All fossil fuels produce carbon dioxide; coal and crude oil also produce sulphur dioxide and nitrogen oxides. As Chapter 12 argued, we must all learn to use less energy, and we should make power stations and other industrial processes more efficient. Industries can reduce sulphur dioxide emission by a process called **scrubbing**, or by a new coal-burning process called **fluidized bed combustion**. This eliminates 90 percent of sulphur dioxide and also reduces nitrogen oxides because the coal burns at a lower temperature. But the technology of fluidized bed combustion is expensive, and it would lead to a large increase in the cost of electricity. Air pollution from **industrial accidents** occasionally causes major health problems. The explosion at the chemical plant in Bhopal, India, in 1986 killed about 4,000 people and caused nerve damage in thousands more (Fig. 1).

Figure 16.1 *Victims of the industrial accident at Bhapal, India in 1986.*

Water pollution from industry can occur intentionally, when factories discharge their effluents directly into rivers, lakes and oceans (see Chapter 8), or unintentionally, when accidents cause leakage of toxic waste into the water supply. Every single day, industrial effluents dump the following waste into the New York estuary: 2,600 metric tons of **carbon**; 870 tons of oil, grease and other **petroleum products**; 520 tons of nitrogen-based **fertilizers**; 230 tons of **iron**; 0.3 tons of **mercury**; and 0.014 tons of **polychlorinated biphenyls** (PCBs). PCBs are byproducts in the production of plastics; they are highly toxic chemicals which enter human tissues via the food chain. Our bodies cannot excrete PCBs; they will continue to build up inside us throughout our lives. Another very toxic waste product is **dioxin**, present in bleached paper products such as disposable diapers, toilet paper and coffee filters. The bleach is only necessary because people expect these products to be white; unbleached "environmentally friendly" toilet paper is a dirty gray color, but is much cleaner in the long term. Factory effluents also discharge large pieces of **solid waste** such as disused machinery, plastic sheets and wire netting. This junk is not only ugly; both animals and ships can become entangled in the debris.

Another pollutant of water is **oil**. Some of it comes from accidents like the Exxon Valdez tragedy (Fig. 2), some from deliberate washing of tanks at sea and some from industrial effluents. Oil coats the feathers of sea birds and the scales of fish. It also has a less visible toxic effect: it reduces the level of oxygen dissolved in the water. Without dissolved oxygen, the sea cannot support any life at all. As well as the fish and seagulls that we can see, oil kills millions of tiny plants and animals in the deeper layers of the ocean. **Acid rain**, discussed in Chapter 7, is another important cause of water pollution and the destruction of aquatic life. Yet another cause is **thermal pollution**. Industries which use water for cooling (such as nuclear power stations) increase the temperature of nearby rivers and lakes by 5–10 degrees. Thermal pollution kills some animals and plants outright. In addition, together with domestic sewage and artificial fertilizers, it promotes overgrowth of bacteria and algae by eutrophication (see Chapter 9) and disrupts the aquatic ecosystem. Industries argue that it would cost too much money to cool the water down before releasing it into the environment.

Figure 16.2 *Clean up of the oil spill from the Exxon Valdez, 1990.*

The pollution of soil with artificial fertilizers and pesticides was discussed in Chapter 9. Soil pollution also occurs when industrial waste is buried or dumped on the land, and via polluted air and water. Sulphur dioxide in the air coats the leaves of plants, blocking out the sun's light and preventing growth. Crop yields are reduced and sulphur accumulates in the soil. The banks of some rivers (such as some sections of the Rhine in Germany) can no longer support the growth of plants because heavy metals and other toxins have entered the soil from the water. It is impossible to remove most of these toxins; in some cases it will take thousands of years for their levels to fall sufficiently for the soil to support life again.

Domestic waste is another environmental problem. "Throwaway" products such as drink cans, plastic bags and disposable diapers are all avoidable sources of domestic waste. When you buy a takeout meal such as a McDonald's hamburger, the packaging often weighs more than the food! Domestic waste is either burned in large **incinerators** or buried in **landfill sites**. Both these processes cause environmental damage. Burning garbage produces carbon dioxide, toxic fumes, soot and other airborne particles as well as an unpleasant smell. Burying garbage in landfill sites can contaminate the soil with toxic products (such as dioxins and PCBs), which then enter the water supply. Human excreta (particularly in disposable diapers) attracts rats and promotes the growth of disease-causing bacteria. Another hazard of landfill sites is the generation of explosive gases, particularly methane, when organic waste decomposes. This is not just a theoretical possibility. In 1986, gas from an old landfill site exploded underneath a house in England and destroyed it. The people who lived in the house did not even know that they were living on a former garbage dump. Other hazards of buried garbage include lead from old pipes and paint, and organic solvents. Children often play on landfill sites because they find the trash sites more interesting than their intended playgrounds; they risk accidents, injuries and poisoning.

When people learn of the irresponsible dumping of industrial waste into rivers and oceans, they are usually horrified. But on a smaller scale, most of us are just as irresponsible with our own waste. About 80 percent of all our domestic waste can be recycled. Most developed countries now have recycling centers for glass, paper, aluminum cans and plastic. But we are often too busy or too lazy to sort our trash for recycling. If we do not change our philosophy of "live now; pay later," our children will bear the burden of our throwaway lifestyle.

Exercises

Summary Writing

Answer the following questions by using the words of the question exactly and in full, and also by referring to the final section of the chapter on domestic waste.

Example: How is domestic waste disposed of?
Answer: Domestic waste is disposed of either in landfill sites or in incinerators.

Now answer the rest of the questions in a similar way.

1 Do the two ways of disposing of waste cause environmental damage?
2 What does burning garbage give off?
3 Are the soil and water supply contaminated when garbage is buried?
4 What are the other dangers of landfill sites?
5 How much domestic waste can be recycled?
6 Do people need to take the trouble to sort their trash?

Write out your sentences to make one paragraph, also using the example given.

a Join the example and sentence 1 with *but* and omit the phrase *of disposing of waste*.
b Begin sentence 5 with *yet* and join sentences 5 and 6 with *but*.
c Give your paragraph a title.

17 Traffic

Pre-reading

Try and answer the following questions. In some cases you'll have to guess! Then check your answers by reading the chapter.

1 The inventor of the motor car was
  - a English.
  - b American.
  - c German.
  - d French.

2 The motor car was invented in
  - a 1875.
  - b 1885.
  - c 1895.
  - d 1905.

3 The biggest cause of air pollution is
  - a industry.
  - b the motor car.
  - c domestic fires.
  - d the burning of domestic waste.

4 Catalytic convertors reduce the emission of carbon dioxide
  - a by 80 percent.
  - b by 50 percent.
  - c by 25 percent.
  - d by nothing.

5 During the rush hour the average speed of traffic in London is
  - a 5 miles per hour.
  - b 11 miles per hour.
  - c 15 miles per hour.
  - d 20 miles per hour.

6 Every year the number of people killed in traffic accidents is
   a 70,000.
   b 150,000.
   c 200,000.
   d 250,000.

7 a 40 percent of all cars are in developed countries.
   b 50 percent of all cars are in developed countries.
   c 60 percent of all cars are in developed countries.
   d 80 percent of all cars are in developed countries.

8 There are more deaths on the roads in developed countries than in developing countries.
   True/False

9 The number of cars in the world doubles every twenty years.
   True/False

10 The main cost of car use is the cost of buying the car in the first place; running it is relatively cheap.
   True/False

In 1885, the German inventor Karl Benz produced the world's first motor car. He probably deserved the fame and fortune that came his way. The motor car dramatically improved the comfort and speed of road transportation, which had previously relied on horses and bicycles. But he could not have predicted the terrible environmental damage that the car would cause. Today, there are over 400 million cars in the world; this number doubles every 20 years. The car is the biggest single cause of air pollution in the world. Almost all cars burn gasoline, which produces carbon dioxide (an important greenhouse gas), nitrogen oxides and hydrocarbons (which react together in sunlight to form ozone), and other toxic products such as benzene and lead. These pollutants were discussed in Chapter 7. Unleaded gasoline is becoming the norm in developed countries. Catalytic convertors, which are now standard features on most new cars, reduce emission of nitrogen oxides and hydrocarbons by up to 90 percent, but they do not reduce carbon dioxide emission. The only way to reduce the carbon dioxide emitted from your car is to drive it less often!

But cars are such a comfortable and convenient way of traveling that car owners usually do not even consider other methods of transportation such as bus, train or bicycle. They do not ask themselves if their journey is really necessary, or if two people could travel in one car — for example, when commuting to work. The private car symbolizes freedom and independence, which are important values in our society. A person's car is often his most important fashion accessory; he uses it to promote a certain image (for example, sporting, sophisticated or cultured) or to demonstrate his wealth. If you can afford a large car, you do not usually buy a small one. The philosophy of the freedom of the individual has a lot to answer for. It underlies unconscious attitudes like "my baby is my baby; everyone else's baby is overpopulation" and "my car is my car; everyone else's car is traffic pollution."

More and more of the countryside is being destroyed every year to make new roads. Many people like to live in the countryside so that they can enjoy the beauty of nature; they drive long distances every day to their work in towns and cities. Paradoxically, many of these people are "environmentally aware" in other ways, but they do not see the connection between their journey to work and the destruction of the environment. Most people who drive to work meet traffic jams at peak times of the day — the "rush hour." The average speed of traffic in the London rush hour is 11 miles per hour, and in certain particularly congested routes it is only two miles per hour. Yet building more roads, or widening existing roads, does not solve the problem because people simply drive their cars more (Fig. 1). An extensive road network encourages people to build amenities such as shopping centers, movie theaters and sports facilities out of town. Instead of bicycling to local stores, we drive five miles to the supermarket and then drive five miles in a different direction to the swimming pool! People without access to a car, including many poor, elderly and disabled people, become second-class citizens, unable to participate fully in society.

Figure 17.1 *Traffic congestion.*

In addition to the problems of air pollution, traffic is bad for health in other ways. Sitting in traffic jams is stressful and probably causes high blood pressure. Driving is a sedentary activity; if people did not own cars they would exercise more, which protects against heart disease. But the most important health hazard associated with traffic is accidents. Worldwide, 250,000 people are killed in accidents every year, and millions more are injured. Traffic accidents are now the most common cause of death in boys and young men in the United States. Eighty percent of all cars are in developed countries, but fatal accidents are 20 times more common per vehicle in developing countries. This is because road surfaces are poor, cars are often old and badly maintained, pedestrians and cyclists are common, and speed limits are not strictly enforced.

The most environmentally-friendly way to travel is to walk or bicycle. The next-best way is to use public transportation. Buses consume less fuel and use less road space per passenger than private cars. They also cause fewer accidents, produce less air pollution, require fewer parking lots and make less noise per passenger. If everyone traveled by public transportation, the bus and train networks would be more economical and could provide a more extensive service. If city centers were less congested with traffic, more people would walk or bicycle. In some countries, such as China, the Netherlands and Denmark, there are extensive networks of bicycle paths, which make cycling a safe and enjoyable form of transportation. These networks have been built because the governments in these countries have consciously decided to encourage the use of the bicycle. Although it costs much less public money to build a bicycle path than to widen a road, most local authorities do not consider bicycle paths as a serious answer to their traffic problems.

As well as encouraging alternative forms of transportation, governments and local authorities should make the use of private cars less convenient and more expensive. Companies should not be allowed tax rebates when they buy new cars for their executives. At present, the major cost of car use is the capital cost of buying the car; after that, the cost per mile traveled is lower than the cost of public transportation in most countries. This phenomenon should be reversed. The tax on gasoline should be increased. Congested roads should have toll gates so that people pay every time they use the road. Cars should be prohibited in downtown areas, shopping streets and other public places. People who travel in car pools (that is, several people sharing a car) should have priority in parking lots or discounts at gas stations. And in the longer term, we should work toward a less car-oriented society in which workplaces, shopping and recreational facilities are within walking or cycling distance of most people's homes.

Exercises

Section A Discussion Work

i) Consider the ideas suggested by the author in the last two paragraphs. How popular would these ideas be in your country? Would it be possible to introduce them? How do you feel about them?

ii) What do you think are the main traffic problems in your country? What should be done about them?

Section B Summary Writing

The following paragraph summarizes the main points made in the last two paragraphs about what should be done now as regards traffic problems. Write out the paragraph and put one word in each of the blank spaces to complete it.

Both local and national government need .... take action to protect the environment .... the destruction caused by the car. .... is best done by public transport, ... bicycle or on foot. If people .... public transport, it would be cheaper, ... better service and more people would .... or cycle in city centers. To .... cars, they should be made more .... to use by increasing the tax .... gasoline and introducing tolls on busy .... Other measures involve banning cars from .... places and encouraging car pools.

18 Poverty and environmental damage

Pre-reading
With your partner look at Graph 1 and discuss what they tell you. Then scan the text quickly to find the paragraph where Graph 1 is discussed and compare your discussion with what the author says.

Poverty creates environmental damage, and environmental damage creates poverty. Six factors contribute to this relationship: population growth, the Third World debt, war, land ownership, the influence of multinational companies and transfer of technology. **Population growth** was discussed in Chapter 2. Poor people have more children than rich people either deliberately (because they fear that some will die) or by accident (because they do not know about contraception). Educated women have fewer and healthier children. In fact, spending money on the education of girls and women is the most cost-effective way to reduce population growth and improve people's general health in a developing country.

Many poor countries owe money to richer countries. This **Third World debt** began in the 1970s. The discovery of new reserves of oil created wealth ("petrodollars") for a few countries, which put their money in international banks. The banks offered very low interest rates to encourage borrowing. Almost every developing country borrowed some money; Mexico and Nigeria took out huge loans. In 1980, interest rates increased because of pressure from the United States. The developing countries became unable to pay their debts. They diverted money to "feed the debt," and poverty and hunger increased. The International Monetary Fund demanded measures such as lower wages and prices, reduced public spending, increased charges for utilities (for example, water supply and sewage disposal), and reduced government food subsidies. In many developing countries, the average income, water quality, infant mortality rate and life expectancy are all worse today than they were 20 years ago. About half a million children die every year as a direct consequence of the Third World debt. The developing countries give more money back as interest on the Third World debt than they receive in "aid" from the richer countries. The national debt of several developing countries is now greater than their gross national product.

What did the developing countries do with the money they borrowed? If you give a poor man a large sum of money, he will probably not spend it sensibly. The developing countries did not spend much money on economic or social developments (such as factories, schools or hospitals), or on food subsidies. Some money went on large-scale water diversion schemes such as dams and hydroelectric plants (see Chapters 8 and 14). Some went on lavish lifestyles for a few rich politicians. But the greatest waste was military expenditure, which increased fivefold between 1970 and 1990; gross national product per head only doubled. In 1992, the average per capita expenditure on arms in the Third World was U.S. $38 (compared with $12 on health). Military expenditure transfers even more money from the Third World to the West. Industrialized countries make sophisticated, high-technology weapons and export them to the poor countries for profit. Most **wars** in the world today occur within or between developing countries. Some national leaders seem to prefer aggression to dialogue. War devastates any country, but its impact is most dramatic in developing countries. Children become orphans; healthy young men and women become cripples; food and water supplies are cut off; houses, schools and hospitals are destroyed; communication systems fail. The people often need large sums of money to rebuild their lives after episodes of pointless violence with neighboring tribes or countries.

If a whole community is near starvation, expressions such as "environmentally friendly" and "sustainable development" will mean nothing to them. Their only food supply may come from using powerful fertilizers on exhausted soil. Their only energy supply may be poor-quality coal burned in an inefficient furnace. Their sewage system may have been destroyed by war, so people must dump their waste in the river. A family's only income may be from selling firewood cut from public forests. The world's poorest people face a choice that richer people will never need to make: their own immediate survival or the long-term survival of the land they inhabit. The fight for survival can make people greedy and dishonest. Bribery and corruption are very common in the Third World. In the 1970s, Bangladesh borrowed money from the international banks to build 3,000 simple tubewells (Fig. 1). The government thought that each tubewell would provide irrigation for about 35 farmers. But almost every tubewell soon became the property of one rich farmer, who bribed local government officials and sold the water to other farmers at an inflated price. The poorest farmers were driven off the land. Instead of easing poverty, the tubewells made it worse. Land ownership is vital to poor farmers in the Third World. But more and more land is becoming concentrated in the hands of a few rich landowners. In Latin America, 93 percent of arable farmland is now owned by 7 percent of farmers. When there is no work, **landless laborers** must beg, starve or migrate. Brazilian peasants, driven off their land, move north into the Amazon rainforests and burn the trees to clear new land for farming.

Figure 18.1 *Tubewell in Bangladesh.*

Large **multinational companies** have great influence over developing countries. The top 500 companies in the world now control about 70 percent of world trade, 80 percent of foreign investment and 30 percent of gross domestic product. The sales budgets of the largest companies are larger than the entire national budget of many poor countries! Multinational companies create jobs, buy raw materials and import technology into developing countries. They can create poverty if they pay low wages or demand cheap prices for commodities. The price of coffee in Costa Rica has fallen dramatically over the past 15 years. Costa Rican peasants are working harder now than ever before, but their wages have never been lower. The multinational companies can also cause — or prevent — massive environmental damage. They can, if they choose, introduce energy-efficient technology, recycling and waste-management policies into developing countries. If they do not, the cycle of poverty, debt and destruction will continue. Perhaps there should be international laws that restrict the activities of multinational companies in the developing world, so that local industry and agriculture can develop. But many economists say that free trade between all countries is essential to the world economy. The General Agreement on Tariffs and Trade (GATT), which was set up in 1947, is an international agreement between different countries to reduce barriers to free trade. Environmentalists argue that GATT will improve free trade but it will also increase both poverty and environmental destruction.

Energy-efficient technology is expensive. It will eventually save money and reduce pollution, but the initial capital expense is high. The developed countries are now reaping the benefits of research into energy efficiency. Our cars use less gasoline and emit less air pollution. Our washing machines use less hot water. Our steel industry uses less coal. Greenhouse gas emissions in the developed world have stabilized and are even beginning to fall. But in Eastern Europe and the former Soviet Union, the governments subsidized energy prices and inefficient industries until very recently. Energy-efficient technology is almost unknown there; pollution levels are high and rising; and the countryside continues to suffer damage. Graph 1 shows that poor countries have a lower carbon dioxide emission per capita than richer countries, but the emission per dollar of gross national product is relatively high. As the energy consumption of newly-industrializing countries rises, the effect on world carbon dioxide levels will be immense. China plans to build 1,000 new fossil fuel power stations in the next 10 years! The rich countries have a moral responsibility to encourage the use of energy-efficient technology throughout the world. But they are not being very helpful. The newest and most efficient technology is still protected by **patent**. This means that the company that invented a particular piece of technology can demand money (**royalties**) if another company copies its ideas. Instead of giving away ideas for energy-efficient technology, the West is *selling* them to the developing countries! These countries pay $160 billion to Western multinational companies in royalties for new technology every year. This is eight times as much as they receive in aid from Western governments.

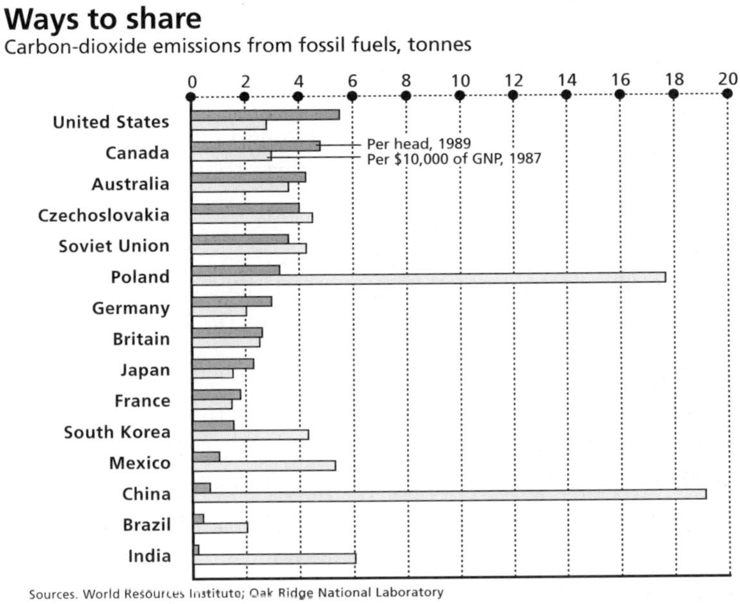

Graph 1 *Carbon dioxide emissions from fossil fuels.*

The environment and world poverty are both political issues. If we care about the environment, we must do more than buy "environmentally friendly" laundry detergent and recycle our newspapers. We must address some of the uncomfortable and complex political questions raised in this chapter. How can we improve the rights of women in the developing world? Should the international banks write off the Third World debt? Should our governments ban the sale of arms to developing countries? Should we stop giving aid to these countries unless they spend it on "suitable" projects? Should the General Agreement on Tariffs and Trade be altered to protect small national economies from exploitation by large multinational companies? While these questions remain unanswered, the developing nations will remain trapped in the downward spiral in which they cause ever more environmental destruction as they get poorer.

Exercises

Section A Discussion Work

Consider in small groups one or more of the important questions raised in the chapter or organize a class debate with two speakers for the motion and two against. Possible motions could be:

1 The sale of arms should be banned to all developing countries.
2 All Third World debt should be cancelled immediately.
3 Multinational companies do more harm than good.

Section B Summary Writing

i) Which paragraph do you think summarizes the complex issues raised in the chapter? Talk about this question with your partner.

ii) The final paragraph answers the question asked in (i). Re-write it putting a correct form of a verb in each of the blank spaces. The verbs to be used are: *to be, to address, to alter, to remain, to ban, to spend, to stop, to write off, to give, to get, to recycle, to cause, to improve, to buy, to care, to do*. Finally, check your paragraph with the one in the chapter.

The environment and world poverty .... both political issues. If we .... about the environment, we must .... more than .... "environmentally friendly" laundry detergent and .... our newspapers. We must .... some of the uncomfortable and complex political questions raised in this chapter. How can we .... the rights of women in the developing world? Should the international banks .... the Third World debt? Should our governments .... the sale of arms to developing countries? Should we .... aid to these countries unless they .... it on "suitable" projects? Should the General Agreement on Tariffs and Trade .... to protect small national economies from exploitation by large multinational companies? While these questions .... unanswered, the developing nations .... trapped in the downward spiral in which they .... ever more environmental destruction as they .... poorer.

19 Cruelty to animals

Pre-reading
In a small group discuss what you think are the main instances of cruelty to animals and draw up a list of examples. Then read the chapter and note down what the author regards as cruelty. Compare your two lists and talk about any differences.

Most of us never question the assumption that human beings have the right to kill animals. We eat them as food, we use their skins to make coats and shoes, and we test drugs and cosmetics on them. Some of us even hunt animals for sport. With our growing awareness of environmental issues, these activities are becoming less acceptable. Deliberate and cruel killing of animals is not a new phenomenon. The people of the Faroe Islands in the Atlantic have probably undertaken their annual cull of pilot whales for centuries (Fig. 1). The cull is a sporting tradition, similar to bullfighting in Spain or fox hunting in Britain. Fewer and fewer people believe that cruelty to animals for sport is justified, particularly when the animal is an endangered species. Shooting tigers in India was once a popular sport for gentlemen; it is now illegal. Killing rare animals for economic gain (**poaching**) is another environmental problem. The black rhinoceros is one of the world's rarest species, with less than 3,000 animals remaining. Two thousand of these are in Zimbabwe, where there is a huge illegal trade in rhino horns. The rhino horn is said to have magical properties. The poachers shoot the rhinos with machine guns and leave them to bleed to death. They smuggle the horns into neighboring countries and sell them. The trade continues despite a worldwide ban on ivory trading and Zimbabwe's shoot-to-kill policy for poachers. The black rhino will be extinct within a few years unless the trade stops.

Figure 19.1 *A pilot whale.*

The use of animals for scientific purposes is a more difficult ethical issue. Many people owe their lives to modern drugs or surgical techniques that were first tested on animals. Some of these developments would not have been possible without animal experiments. People who campaign for animal rights are usually young and healthy, and have not yet needed the benefits of medical progress. Is killing an animal morally equivalent to killing a human being? A few years ago in the United States, there was an interesting legal case. A yacht capsized and two of the sailors fell into the water. The third sailor got into a lifeboat with his dog. Later, he was charged with manslaughter because he did not throw the dog overboard in order to save the two humans. The judge found the sailor not guilty of manslaughter — but would you agree with him?

Perhaps it is ethically acceptable to sacrifice animals for the sake of medical research, as long as the animals do not suffer. But that theoretical standpoint raises two difficult questions: first, what counts as medical research and second, what counts as suffering? Some animal research leads directly to the development of important new drugs that save hundreds of lives. But what if the research concerns only a minor painkiller or a new laxative? And what about the testing of cosmetics on animals? Do all caged animals suffer, or do they suffer only when they are overcrowded, hungry or in pain? Rabbits are often kept in laboratories because the antibodies in their blood are used for immunological research. The scientists have a strong motive to keep the rabbits alive and healthy. Rabbits are expensive to replace, and a new rabbit might not produce the same range of antibodies in its blood. The animals do not seem to suffer, and the scientists say that they have a better (and longer) life than many animals in the wild. But their life is very "unnatural," and the animals are, perhaps, deprived of their dignity. They might also be instinctively afraid of the human beings who look into their cages.

The killing of animals for food causes a lot of avoidable suffering. In **factory farms**, animals are reared purely for the economic value of their meat. The farms are designed to achieve maximum productivity and a fast rate of growth. Living conditions are cramped and uncomfortable. Cows, pigs and chickens are usually kept indoors, with little or no light. Some animals are chained up for most or all of the day. Chickens can go blind from the ammonia fumes produced by their own excrement. Sometimes young calves develop deformities in their joints because there is not enough room for them to exercise. The animals are taken to slaughterhouses in overcrowded trucks (Fig. 2). They are often frightened by this experience; some of them die of shock on the journey. The more brutal methods of killing animals in slaughterhouses have now been banned in many countries. The animals should receive a quick electric shock to stun them before they are killed with a knife. But this does not always work and many animals still die a painful, slow and terrifying death. When people learn of the horrific conditions in factory farms and slaughterhouses, they may decide to become vegetarian. Vegetarians eat no meat; most of them will only buy free-range eggs (that is, eggs laid by chickens that are not kept in cages). They often do not wear leather shoes or carry leather bags. There are, of course, good economic reasons for becoming vegetarian, which are discussed in Chapter 10.

Figure 19.2 *Animals being taken to a slaughterhouse.*

The fur trade is another industry where animals suffer needlessly. Four hundred million animals, including foxes, raccoons, sables and ermine, are killed every year for their coats. Most of them die in traps in North America, Russia and Scandinavia. The trap ensnares one of the animal's legs. The animal lies helpless and in pain for several days until the trapper arrives to kill it. It may try to bite off its own leg in order to escape. The fur trade also has factory farms where animals such as mink and Arctic foxes are kept in dark, cramped conditions until they are killed. Most vegetarians refuse to buy or wear fur coats, and many non-vegetarians also boycott garments made of real fur. The campaign against the fur trade has been so successful that real fur has gone out of fashion and many companies which sold expensive fur coats have gone out of business.

The major religions of the Far East, such as Hinduism and Buddhism, teach that all living things are equal in the eyes of God. They emphasize respect for all forms of animal life, and responsibility for animal welfare. Most Hindus and Buddhists are vegetarian. The religions of the Middle East and the West, such as Islam, Judaism and Christianity, have a different philosophy. They certainly do not condone cruelty to animals, but they believe that God put animals on the earth for man's use. Most Moslems, Jews and Christians are meat-eaters. Their religious festivals include the killing and eating of animals.

Exercises

Summary Writing

Below is a list of the basic points the author makes about cruelty to animals. Using the points, complete the framework provided so that you write a summary in a paragraph.

1 More people are against cruelty to animals in sports, such as fox-hunting.
2 They are particularly against cruel poaching of rare animals.
3 Using animals for essential, life-saving research in medicine is perhaps acceptable if they do not suffer.
4 It is difficult always to know what is suffering for animals.
5 Killing animals for food causes a great deal of unnecessary suffering, as does rearing them in factory farms.
6 The same unnecessary suffering is true for the fur trade.

Nowadays more and more people are.................................... ...., such as fox-hunting and particularly against .... As regards using animals .... if they .... Yet it is difficult .... However, rearing animals .... and killing them for food cause .... This is also ....

20 Sustainable development

Pre-reading

1 What do you think "sustainable development" means?

a Development that can continue without affecting the environment.

b Development that shouldn't be accepted at all because it badly damages the environment.

c Development that is an improvement on the present situation, but damages the environment to some extent.

Check your answer by quickly scanning the first two paragraphs of the chapter.

2 In a small group discuss what the individual can do to help the environment nowadays. Make a list of points. Then quickly find the paragraph where the author suggests what the individual can do and compare your ideas with hers.

This book began by saying that the state of the environment today has reached a crisis point. Unfortunately, it does not end with an easy answer to that crisis. The crisis stems largely from humankind's attempts at "development" — that is, our efforts to make our lives more sophisticated, more comfortable and more satisfying. Development includes **technological** changes (such as the industrial revolution in the 19th century and today's electronic revolution), **social** changes (such as an increase in the division of labor and the separation of the home from the workplace) and **economic** changes (such as the change from subsistence farming to cash crops, the increase in taxation by central governments and the introduction of banks so that people can save or borrow money). All these changes are sometimes called "progress," but as previous chapters in this book have shown, they can have devastating effects on the environment.

Some people have decided to turn their back on any form of development. The teepee people in Wales live in simple tents and farm the surrounding countryside without artificial fertilizers or motorized machinery. They are self-sufficient in food and clothing, they do not use money; and they recycle all their waste. They are also pacifists — that is, they try to live in harmony with one another as well as with the environment. The teepee people have made great personal sacrifices, and they are an important example to all of us. But the primitive, "back to nature" lifestyle of a group of idealistic hippies will never achieve a global solution to the world's environmental crisis. Most realistic environmentalists today aim for **sustainable development** — that is, development that does not damage the environment and which, theoretically, could continue indefinitely. Sustainable development requires action on four levels: by individuals, local authorities, national governments and the international community.

Perhaps the most important contribution an individual can make is to have fewer children. We can also adopt lifestyles that emit less pollution, use less energy and create less waste. We should walk or bicycle rather than travel by car. We should insulate our houses and become less dependent on electrical labor-saving devices. We should avoid "disposable" paper and plastic products such as tableware, handkerchiefs and diapers (Fig. 1) and we should recycle all our metal, glass and paper waste. As consumers, we should become less dependent on manufactured goods in general, since a high proportion of industrial pollution comes from the manufacture of short-lived consumer goods. We should buy "environmentally friendly" products such as unbleached toilet paper, organically-grown vegetables and unleaded gasoline. In addition, perhaps we should try to develop a taste for art, music and literature rather than fashionable clothes, videos and sports cars!

Figure 20.1 *Reusuable diapers.*

Local authorities can promote sustainable development through better planning of towns and cities. Each town should be small enough to feed its population from the surrounding countryside, and should rely as much as possible on local industry. A high proportion of all traffic pollution today is caused by trucks carrying food from one end of a country to another, or by company representatives carrying samples of inessential consumer goods. Local authorities should discourage the use of motor vehicles in towns by prohibiting cars in shopping districts, building public amenities within walking distance of residential areas, and creating bicycle paths instead of more roads. Trees and flowers in public parks make a town more pleasant and also help to counteract the greenhouse effect. Local authorities should provide recycling centers and other collection points for recyclable waste. They should also invest in the technology for disposing of human waste responsibly, rather than simply pouring raw sewage into the sea. The human waste in Calcutta, India, is channeled into the lakes around the city where it fertilizes the growth of aquatic plants. The fish that feed on these plants are an important source of food for the population of Calcutta. This is a good example of sustainable development in practice.

National governments can promote sustainable development through legislation, and through policies on agriculture, energy, transportation and trade. Chapter 12 discussed the **carbon tax**, which makes individuals and industries pay for the carbon dioxide they produce. But this tax will only change people's behavior if the financial penalties are very severe. If energy-efficient technology actually made an industrial process cheaper, all industries would install such technology. If gasoline were 10 or 100 times more expensive, we would all have a strong incentive not to use our cars. The carbon tax today is so small that most people do not know that it exists. Other taxes that national governments could impose include a **tropical hardwood tax** (see Chapter 4) and a **"polluter pays" tax**, in which industries pay a heavy fine for dumping their effluents into the waterways. Unfortunately, governments are usually more interested in winning the next election than in protecting the environment through unpopular taxes.

National agricultural policies should encourage organic farming and discourage the use of fertilizers and pesticides. Central governments should fund more research into renewable energy sources, and stop subsidizing the nuclear power industry. Governments in developed countries should prohibit the export of toxic chemicals, obsolete technology and military weapons to developing countries, and discourage the import of cheap, useless consumer goods. They should guarantee a fair price for imports of staple foodstuffs (such as tea and coffee), and discourage imports of exotic foods (such as pineapples and avocados) in order to encourage a return to sustainable subsistence farming in the Third World. The price of imported beef for the hamburger industry should reflect the true cost of producing the meat — including the cost of replanting forests.

Many of the most complex problems of the environment today demand collaboration between countries. The United Nations Conference on Environment and Development in Rio de Janeiro, 1992, produced a document known as **Agenda 21**, which is an international agreement for working toward sustainable development. It covers issues such as population control, food and agricultural policy, waste disposal and financial aid for conservation projects in developing countries. But Agenda 21, like many documents produced at UNCED, is no more than a list of recommendations, which each country may adopt at its own pace. The failure of UNCED to produce legally binding agreements on these and other environmental issues is one of the biggest failings of international diplomacy this century.

When we look at the world's environmental problems on a global scale, it is hard to believe that any action by one person, one small community or even one whole country, will make any difference. But we should remember the ancient Chinese proverb that says that a journey of a thousand miles begins with a single step. It is time for all of us to take that first step, before it is too late.

Exercises

Summary Writing

Answer the following questions by using the words of the question exactly and in full, and also by referring to the chapter.

Example: How many levels of action are required to achieve sustainable development?

Answer: Four levels of action are required to achieve sustainable development.

Now answer the remaining questions in a similar way.

1 What do these levels relate to?
2 What is perhaps the best thing the individual can do?
3 Should the individual also have a lifestyle that causes less pollution, uses less energy and creates less waste?
4 Should local authorities improve the planning of towns and cities in many different ways?
5 Should the state pass laws to change policies on agriculture, energy, transportation and trade?
6 Are cooperation and action needed between countries?
7 Are many environmental problems on a global scale?

Write out your sentences to make one paragraph, also using the example given.

a Join the example and sentence 1 with *which*.
b Join sentences 2 and 3 with *and*. Replace the individual in sentence 3 with *he*.
c Join sentences 4 and 5 with *and*.
d Join sentences 6 and 7 with *as* and begin the new sentence with the phrase *at the international level*.
e Give your paragraph a title.